My
PEACHY
CITY

Printed in the United States of America

Edited by Raymond McAlwee
Cover and book design by Denise McDonald

First Printing, 2017

ISBN 9780-578-19124-951895

Rose Garden Press
3510 Claremont Street
Baltimore, MD 21224

MY
PEACHY
CITY

A Story of The Iconic People and Places of Baltimore

To Brandon Soderberg

Have a great summer

By

Leonora "Peachy" Dixon

Best wishes
Love
Peachy

6/19/17

ACKNOWLEDGMENTS

I'd like to acknowledge all the kind owners, managers and employees of the following famous Baltimore establishments who have allowed me to include their businesses in "My Peachy City." They are a big part of the pride that I and my fellow citizens and neighbors feel for all their contributions to our city.

Sabatino's

Domino Sugar

H & S Bakery

The Baltimore Sun

The Maryland Jockey Club

The Baltimore Orioles

The Baltimore Ravens

Johns Hopkins University and Hospital Medical Center

United book Press

Under Armour

Go Daddy

My daughter Anna Maria & her husband Dave Carpenter

My granddaughter Christy & her husband Tom Strawser

My granddaughter Erin & her husband Anthony Stapleton

My granddaughter Rachel

My daughter Michelle Lloyd

My granddaughter Liz and her husband Ricky Gondeck

My grandson Jonathan and his wife Hope Esser

My brother Vincent Di Pietro

My sister Rosie & her husband Bernie Jubb

My Deep Appreciation to:

Ron Daniels

Josh Charles

Carol & Stanley Alpert

Sharon Miller & Lenny Wachs

Renee Sherman & Hillard Folus

Kathy Koenig & Bobby Schunck

Malinda & Linda Davis

Lori Smith

Michael & Susie Olesker

Father Bob Albright & Jim & Sandra Hintenach

Dr. Michael Sanow

Sherrie Szchalski

My bosses Vincent Culotta & Renato Rotundo

My editor Raymond McAlwee

My book designer Ms. Denise McDonald

Mr. Bill Hendrix and United Book Press

My
BALTIMORE

CHAPTER ONE

Hello. Let me tell you a little story about the wonderful town I live in – Baltimore. We had the best Mayor anyone could ever have to take care of our town. His name was Mayor William Donald Schaefer. He had the amazing insight to improve Baltimore by making all the courageous moves possible to accomplish his goal. His transformation of the dilapidated harbor into the magnificent jewel Baltimore City is today was unbelievable. I was only one person among many fortunate people to have known him.

The Early Days of the Inner Harbor

During this period of time the harbor was hardly a place anyone wanted to visit. The harbor was called Smith Park then. It was just a field on Light Street with rotting warehouses and piers. There was a fish market downtown right were Ruth's Chris restaurant is located today.

The only thing Baltimore was known for was the infamous "Block." This is where the famous Blaze Star performed nightly. When visitors came to Baltimore from out of town on business, they wanted to visit the famous Block. The Block had many strip clubs, and was known all over America.

Blaze Starr was known all the way to California for her special strip tease acts. While she was on the stage, she did many funny antics. She really didn't strip all the way. She gave the illusion of making it look like she stripped. This was why men kept coming back. It was the illusion that kept the men wanting to see her more.

Another bar at the Harbor was Elmer's Musical Bar on the corner of Light and Pratt Streets. It was a family owned business. It was located on a dark, desolate corner in downtown Baltimore. It was a motorcycle bar which had two doors. One night a biker rode his bike through one door and out the other. Elmer and his wife Rose worked the business together.

Albert Greenwald was Elmer's brother. Albert sold produce in the morning. When he went to buy produce, he would stop at his brother's bar to visit him. When Elmer and his wife Rose closed their bar in the evening, they were hungry and wanted something to eat. The only place open at this time was Sabatino's. They frequently visited the restaurant late at night because everyone in Baltimore went there. It was the place to go when the bars closed to get some good food.

Mr. Greenwald sold produce to many local grocery stores in Baltimore. One of his customers was Eddie's Super Market located in the Erdman Shopping Center. Eddie's was owned by Irvin Levy. Ironically, my cousin Tom Tana and my boss Vince Culotta from Sabatino's worked there when they were young, and they became friends.

During the time Mayor Thomas D'Alesandro the third was the Mayor, riots broke out in the City. He was beside himself. He couldn't believe these awful things were happening to the city during this time on his watch. The riots left young Tommy very distraught. Even though his father Tommy D'Alesandro, Jr. served Baltimore City as Mayor for several years, young Tommy did not want to seek another term in office.

William Donald Schaefer loved the city of Baltimore very much. He wanted the job of Mayor more than anything. He was the City Council President at this time. He didn't want to take anything away from Tommy. Before he went to apply for Mayor, he made sure young Tommy D'Alesandro was not going to run again. Mr. Schaefer couldn't believe this opportunity was coming his way. He immediately went down to the Board of Elections where his friend Gene Raynor worked. Mr. Schaefer filled out the application to become Mayor.

Schaefer had the most fantastic personality. He was tall and a little on the heavy side with a receding hair line. He could convince anyone to go along with his ideas. When he made his inaugural speech he declared cities are the strength of America. He said, "It is the cities that make the idea, which sets the tempo for its growth."

Schaefer lived in the city all of his life in his parent's home. It was located on the west side of Baltimore. While he lived there, people asked him to fix things that needed to be repaired in the neighborhood. He always helped his neighbors out. Because of his genuine assistance to the people in his neighborhood, he received the majority of the African American votes.

Even though his opponent was a black man, Schaefer won. Everyone liked William Donald Schaefer, because they believed he was a sincere individual. He had the aggressive attitude to get the job done.

Mayor Schaefer speaking at the1980 Police Expo

The New Mayor's Outlook

After William Donald Schaefer became Mayor, he was so enthusiastic about having a City Fair. He wanted people to come back into the city. He realized if the people didn't come and visit the city, he wouldn't have the resources to accomplish his agenda. He needed help putting his idea together. He started to involve all the big businesses that were located in Baltimore to become active participants in his projects.

When Mayor Schaefer started the City Fair, it created jobs for many people. Mayor Schaefer was the person who brought the rebirth back to the Inner Harbor. The City Fair made people aware of all the good things Mayor Schaefer was doing for the City of Baltimore. He would say, "We have got to show our love for the City and one another."

He got people from different neighborhoods actively involved in making the City Fair a neighborhood affair. Mayor Schaefer changed the once rat infested harbor into one of the most marvelous tourist attractions on the east coast. The water in the harbor was dirty and not inviting for people to come down and visit. Mayor Schaefer changed all of this. He improved the Inner Harbor. He made it more attractive and inviting for people to want to come downtown. When the people came downtown they brought money back into the city. This was the main incentive Mayor Schaefer had in mind.

Because of the City Fair, all the other ethnic groups branched out and had their own festivals at the Inner Harbor. The festivals consisted of the Italians, Greeks, Polish, German, African Americans, and Jewish. Each of these festivals attracted more than a million people to the Inner Harbor every year. These festivals were held all summer long, which kept people constantly coming to the Inner Harbor. Mayor Schaefer was on a mission to change people's attitudes about Baltimore City. When he made all the improvements to the Inner Harbor, it helped him to accomplish his goal. The Inner Harbor became the showplace of Baltimore City. In 1976, the Tall Ships came to Baltimore. The ships attracted thousands of people to come down to the Inner Harbor. Because of all the excitement happening in Baltimore during this time, it enticed me to become involved in the festivals at the Inner Harbor.

One of Mayor Schaefer's Fans

John Westbrook was one of the architects who helped to design the Inner Harbor and was a friend with Dr. Norberto Machiran. When Dr. Machiran moved here from Cuba, he thought the city was dirty and not inviting for people to come and visit. After Mr. Westbrook and his crew of associates designed the construction of the Inner Harbor, he made it the showplace it is today. Dr. Machiran was so impressed at the changes happening at the Inner Harbor. He wanted to congratulate Mayor Schaefer on his wonderful achievement. Dr. Machiran was finally able to meet Mayor Schaefer at the Latino Festival held at Martin's West. There Dr. Machiran told Mayor Schaefer how much he appreciated the wonderful transformation he made to the Inner Harbor.

Connolly's Seafood

The Mayor had many friends. One of his friends was Mr. Connolly. He owned Connolly's Seafood restaurant located in the Inner Harbor on Pratt Street. Mayor Schaefer loved the food at Connolly's and he ate there three or four times a week. The Mayor and Mr. Connolly were like brothers. They discussed the politics of the day and aired their differences.

Mr. Connolly had such a way about him; he was a congenial person and he got along well with his customers and his employees. Mr. Connolly had his waitresses dress in costumes on Halloween. His daughter Karen made the costumes for the waitresses to wear. My friend Mary Giorgilli was a waitress during this time and wore many different costumes on Halloween. Mayor Schaefer always commented on all the costumes the waitresses wore. Boats were docked near Connolly's restaurant on Pratt Street. They sold oysters and watermelons. Every summer my father would go to the harbor to buy watermelons

Mary Giorgilli at Connolly's Restaurant

from the boats docked there. This was one of the treats my father gave to us during the summer months.

Thomas D'Alesandro Jr.

Before Schaefer or Tommy D'Alesandro, III, there was Thomas D'Alesandro, Jr. He was an American politician. He left school at the age of thirteen to help support his family. Later he attended Calvert Business College in Baltimore. He was an insurance broker. He remained in his community in a modest row home. When asked why he never left Little Italy, he replied, "I'm a Paisano. These are my people and this is where I belong." His parents were from Abruzzo, Italy, the same place my father's family was from in Italy.

He was elected to serve on the Baltimore City Council from 1935 to 1938. He was elected to the 76 U.S. Representatives from Maryland's 3rd congressional district. He served four consecutive terms in Congress, from January 3, 1939 to May 16, 1947.

While he was in Congress, he strongly supported the Bergson Group. He challenged the Roosevelt Administration's Policies on the Jewish refugee issue during the Holocaust. He later lobbied against the British control of Palestine. This was despite his equally strong support for Roosevelt's other policies.

Mr. D'Alesandro was married to Annunciata Lombardi. The couple had six children, five sons and a daughter. His wife, along with their daughter Nancy, worked the phones during many elections to help Tommy Senior win his many elections. Even though Nancy was young, she helped her mother with all the phone calls. Nancy later went into politics and became the Speaker of the House now known as Nancy Pelosi.

D'Alesandro was the Mayor of Baltimore, Maryland for twelve years from 1947 to 1959. Baseball fans will always have a special place in their hearts for Mayor D'Alesandro. In 1953, he, along with Clarence Miles, succeeded in having major league baseball return to the city. The city lost the franchise fifty years earlier. The St. Louis Browns were transferred to the city and opened the 1954 season as the Baltimore Orioles. He was known as "Tommy" to his constituents and to Presidents Roosevelt, Truman, and Kennedy.

The Sun Paper called him the building Mayor. His accomplishments included the opening of Friendship Airport, the 17 mile Baltimore Harbor Tunnel in 1957, and the building of Memorial Stadium.

He launched the urban renewal projects and the Charles Center project. He fought for the elimination of old waterfront wharves at Pratt and Light Streets. This was known as Sam Smith National Park which today is the home of Harbor Place.

He overcame his phobia of air travel to accompany President Truman on an inaugural flight into Baltimore's new airport in 1950. He tried out the harbor's new radar-control system in 1949. He used the ship-to-shore equipment on his own 46-foot cruiser in rain and fog. He snipped the ribbon for a new heliport in 1958. He helped establish the Maryland Port Authority in 1956.

After the Mayor completed all these projects the voters backed him for a third four-year term in 1955. There was several accusations brought against him about municipal corruptions. Several indictments resulted; he was not involved. Then the party began to turn its back on him. The party ousted him from the state's Democratic National Committee. He held this post for four years. Then he lost his re-nomination as Mayor to J. Harold Grady.

One of his most controversial episodes in City Hall was his support of a tax on newspaper advertising. This was the first such levy in the country. He won the fight for the tax but he lost his rebid for Mayor.

Mayor Clarence Du Burns recalled under Mr. D'Alesandro, the city built eighty-seven new schools. He provided new facilities for black students who had to relocate to inferior segregated buildings. He was 84 years old when he passed away due to cardiac arrest. It was a Sunday at Mercy Hospital's coronary intensive care unit. He was survived by his wife, four sons, one daughter, sixteen grandchildren, and one great-grandchild.

The Tall Ships Bicentennial in1976

Uncle Mimi (second from left), at a Baltimore City Council Event

Chapter Two

The First City Fair

Mr. Robert Embory was in charge of the Housing Commission, and he was trying to get people to come back into the City. His ideas finally got to three people, Hope Quackenbush, Sandy Hillman, and Chris Hartman. These people put their heads together and sold the idea of the first Baltimore City Fair which was held in Charles Center.

Mr. Hartman and Mr. Webster were in charge of the Housing and Community developing committee. They started to visit all the different neighborhoods. They tried to get people from the different ethnic groups to display what their neighborhoods were famous for.

Everyone told them you can't do this. No one will come. If they do come there will be riots. People couldn't stop remembering what happened in 1968. To the surprise of everyone, the Baltimore City Fair took place without a hint of any disaster.

The first City Fair was held in Charles Center which had a huge statue of Mayor Thomas D'Alesandro, Jr. Tommy D'Alesandro, III was his son. Young Tommy stood on a platform located in Charles Center and announced the official opening of the 1970 Baltimore City Fair. There were 340,000 people attending the first Baltimore City Fair.

As the weekend fair was supposed to start, a huge storm called David marched right through downtown Baltimore. It tore down all the exhibits and booths. The storm left debris all over the place. Despite this awful storm that destroyed the stands and the exhibits, it brought people together. The people who had stands helped each other out to fix their booths so the fair could go on. The huge storm brought people together more than anyone could have imagined. This was the thing Mr. Embory and his associates wanted to happen all along. People from all different ethnic groups, from east, west, north, and south emerged downtown.

This was the first City Fair held downtown, and no one knew what to expect. After all the skepticism, when everyone expected the worst, it turned out to be a fabulous affair. The first year the Baltimore City Fair, was run by all volunteers, who did not receive a salary. The Fair was also based on credit only. When the first year turned out to be such an enormous success, there was no trouble obtaining money from the banks to run the next fair. Everyone wanted to enter the fair the following year.

The City Fair was moved from the Charles Center to the Harbor on Pratt and Light Street and across Key Highway. During this period the Inner Harbor was a place of deterioration, rotting piers and dilapidated warehouses. There were some seedy bars and an old power generating station, and rats.

Mr. Earl Arnett, a columnist for *The Baltimore Sun* said, "The Baltimore City Fair helped neighborhoods to unite in a time when there was much distrust in the City. The neighborhoods brought life back into the City."

The spirit that started the first Baltimore City Fair was one which lasted for many years. What it highlighted was the bringing together of all the different neighborhoods. In turn, it also brought all different types of people closer together. This was Mayor Schaefer's whole idea in the first place to get people to come downtown to the city, and boy... how it worked.

The Baltimore City Fair

The Baltimore City Fair had many exhibits, craft people, and artisans. There were iron workers, engravers, toymakers, quilt makers, and stained glass makers. There were puppet shows, clowns, and jugglers. It had rides of all kinds, and the children loved going on the rides, including my children.

All the different stages had celebrities performing on them. Here are some of the people who appeared at the City Fair: The Baltimore Symphony Orchestra, Marilyn McCoo and Billy Davis, Jr., The Zim Zemarel band, Diahann Carroll, Cab Calloway, Lionel Hampton, Fats Domino, Al Madman Baitch, The Platters, Billy Eckstine, The Benny Goodman

Orchestra, Buddy Rich, The Glen Miller Orchestra, and Tony Randall also appeared.

Mr. Karl Wallenda, a 68 year old circus performer walked a tight rope 60 feet above the Baltimore harbor. It was a 15 minute walk. People watched this exciting event from all over the Inner Harbor. Mr. Wallenda performed his tight rope act without a hitch before the City Fair began.

The First Fireworks at the Harbor

Mayor Schaefer planned to have a New Years Eve Celebration at the harbor. Mayor Schaefer had a way about him. He could easily get people to do whatever he wanted them to do. At the request of Mayor Schaefer, Deputy Commissioner Bataglia did what the Mayor wanted. This celebration has turned into a gala celebration every New Years Eve. The year this began was 1970.

Because the Mayor was planning to have this celebration, he needed someone to sell food there. This was the first time the City did anything like this. No one knew how many people would attend the event. The event started around 9 o'clock until 12:30.

My good friends Elsie and Vince Protani had a business on Frankford Avenue; in the shopping center known as the Columbia Center. Their business was near the Red Rooster, which was a popular spot for young people during this time. The Protani's were there for eight to nine years. They belonged to the Belair Road Lodge of the Sons of Italy which had turned into the America Vespucci Lodge.

Deputy Commissioner Bataglia knew the Protani's because of their involvement in the Sons of Italy. He came into their shop to ask them if they would have a stand at the harbor. The Commissioner wanted them to do this for New Year's Eve. This meant the Protani's only had one week to prepare for the affair.

The Protani's thought the Mayor and the Commissioner was a little crazy because no one ever sold food at the Harbor on New Year's Eve before. Their stand was where the Science Center is now. The tide came up to their stand. Elsie thought they were going to be flooded out. Thankfully the water never reached their stand. During this period in time, Harbor Place was not the beautiful showplace it is today.

The fireworks were a beautiful exhibition, and a large crowd came down to the harbor to see them. To the surprise of Elsie and Vince, they sold out of all the food they had brought for the event. Vince was so happy he grabbed Elsie and gave her a big kiss for New Year's Eve which surprised Elsie. They tried to sell pickle herring because it is supposed to stand for good luck on the New Year. The people who came to the celebration at the Harbor were young and didn't know what it was for. Therefore the herring did not go over at all.

Carol Channing was in town doing her show, "The Bed before Yesterday." The commissioner asked her to sing during the New Year's Eve Celebration. She was so close to the Protani's stand, they could hear her sing. The next year Bataglia asked the Protani's to participate in the Fire Works Celebration again. This year they moved the event closer to Pratt and Light Streets. The planning committee thought it would be a better spot to sell food.

Thousands of people came to the New Year's celebration. Because of the large turnout, this event became a magnificent affair. The crowds were larger than the year before. The Protani's were so busy they ran out of rolls and they had to sell the hot dogs and meatballs on sticks. It was unbelievable.

Because the first year was such a success, many other vendors started to sell food at the New Year's Eve Celebration. At one time the people were standing eight deep to buy food. There wasn't enough food to serve all the people. Many people were upset because of this. They left the Harbor before midnight and missed the entire fireworks display.

Carnival

While becoming more involved with the Sons of Italy, I met two of the most influential people in my life, Vince and Elsie Protani. They helped me through many of my endeavors. These two wonderful people advised me through most of my career, and we are still friends today.

Before the Italian festivals started there was "the Carnival." It was a celebration held in South America and many European Countries. The

Carnival was held at the Fifth Regiment Armory. This was a huge celebration before Ash Wednesday, the beginning of Lent. It was similar to the celebration they hold in New Orleans during the Mardi Gras. The Italians sold food, drinks, and crafts at the Carnival. Elsie and Vince Protani helped me get a stand in the Carnival. This helped me get more involved in the Sons of Italy.

Elsie and I sold crafts and Pizzelle cookies. The food vendors became upset because I was on the side to sell crafts only. Finally I convinced the people in charge I was only selling them there. After I explained this, they were okay. Elsie and I had a good time there. Even though we didn't sell much of our products, it was a learning experience for me.

I wanted to be in the fairs held at the Inner Harbor and this helped me to do this. The Protani's informed me where to rent the equipment and gas for the festival. They were a great help to me through my life.

Dancers at the Italian Festival

Helen Bentley with Mayor Schaefer

Helen Bentley

Chapter Three

Helen Delich Bentley

In 1984, Helen Bentley was elected to serve the first of her five terms representing Maryland's 2nd Congressional District. She developed a reputation as a skilled mediator between labor and management. She was an energetic advocate for jobs and economic opportunity. She also was an internationally recognized expert on maritime issues. Bentley pushed for fair trade and a strong national defense.

Mrs. Bentley laid the groundwork for the establishment of the Maritime Security which provided adequate funding for American Flagged Cargo Ships. Today this program has salvaged a major remnant of America's merchant marines. Her passion in life was to preserve and promote her adopted hometown port. She was gruff, but she spoke out relentlessly in her unmistakable gravelly voice against anyone that threatened the port.

Helen wanted to leave her small town in Nevada. She earned a bachelor's degree in three years at the University of Missouri. She wrote to every newspaper in the East to ask for a reporter job. This was her ambition to always be a reporter, although she didn't want one on the society page. Helen got a telegram from *The Baltimore Sun* paper in 1945 offering a reporter job. She became a maritime reporter for the Port of Baltimore's beat. She was soon belting out a regular column entitled "Around the Waterfront." She had never seen a ship or the ocean before this job. It was a tough, male-dominated environment, but she loved it.

Helen said women have to be willing to work and produce and not expect favors because they are women. She also said she had to be as mean and tough as she could be. Helen was thrown out of many union halls. She was kicked out and carried out. But soon the union bosses realized she was their friend. She was always fair and honest.

One time a longshoreman made a disparaging comment about her nose; she slugged him. She had to deal with the male colleagues in the newsroom. They constantly picked on her. She always had to fight back and that's how she learned all the dirty words. She had a mouth like a longshoreman. She was the hardest working reporter out there. People respected her because they knew she was honest. In 1950 she married William Roy Bentley. She met him on a blind date. She told people she didn't know why he agreed to marry her.

Soon she moved into television. For fifteen years she turned out weekly thirty minute segments for her series. It was called, "The Port that built a City." She produced, directed, edited, wrote, and did interviews for her series. She broadcasted from aboard ship. She brought on sailors and stevedores as guests. She made her producers nervous. Helen could cuss like any Marine. She could out-drink any two longshoremen. While she had this program she still covered maritime and edited all the maritime copies at the *Sun*. She brought the attention of the public and government to see the economic impact the port had on Maryland.

In 1969 Helen was appointed by President Richard Nixon to be the highest ranking woman of Nixon's administration. She served in a key governmental position in the maritime field. She was the principal architect in the 1970 Merchant Marine Act to establish a level of government support for building tankers and bulk carriers in U.S. shipyards. She used her chairmanship to fight in Congress against the transfer of jobs overseas.

Her coverage of the supply problem for American's war effort in Vietnam, led to the institution of containers. They were the preferred method of cargo transportation. Bentley used her chairmanship as a platform to strengthen American industry. She continued the fight in Congress. She led the fight against transferring of jobs overseas.

She knew the dredging of the Chesapeake Bay to a depth of 50 feet could accommodate large ships to come into the harbor. Many people objected to the dredging of the Chesapeake Bay. The people of Hart-Miller Island were the people who most objected to this.

When she couldn't convince anyone of this, she entered elective politics in 1980 as a Republican. She tried three times to win and finally on her third try she won. This was after Ronald Reagan's landslide election.

She began a decade in Congress. She shared the same style as Barbara Mikulski. She was gruff and tough. She convinced the blue collar conservative Democrats to vote with her.

While she was in Congress, she worked like hell. She punched through legislation to open islands to dredging. This would ensure the channel to allow larger ships to continue up the bay. She was friends with William Donald Schaefer. Baltimore was known as the port that wouldn't work in the rain. This angered Mr. Schaefer. Ms. Bentley asked him to let her mediate with the association. He agreed and she got the rain clause eliminated. She never butted heads with Mr. Schaefer. When he died she was devastated.

Mrs. Bentley was also a good friend to my uncle Dominic Mimi DiPietro. They worked together on many projects for the port of Baltimore, Maryland. She also attended his funeral.

Mrs. Bentley has christened 16 American flag ships. In 1987 at Baltimore's Bethlehem Steel Shipyard, she christened and named five ships. She always told it the way she saw it. She spent nearly two decades on the docks interviewing tugboat captains and longshoremen.

Ralph Galliano was the editor of the *SFPPR News and Analysis*. He said Bentley was the Trumpian of her day. She was a true American who worked hard for working men and women everywhere. She cursed you to your face, but she'd never stab anyone in the back.

In June of 2006 Governor Robert Ehrlich announced he had officially renamed Baltimore's port as "The Helen Delich Bentley Port of Baltimore." Mr. Ehrlich hailed Mrs. Bentley as "the godmother of the port." Mrs. Bentley received a standing ovation. She was speechless. Mr. Ehrlich said, "It was the only time he ever shut her up."

My helper and me at the Italian Festival

Maryland State Senator Joseph Bonvegna, My Uncle Mimi Di Pietro, Mayor Donald Schaefer, and House of Delegates Louis V. Cavallaro

Chapter Four

Working the Fairs

The City Fair kept getting bigger and better every year, especially after Mayor Schaefer started to improve the Inner Harbor. More people were coming down to the Inner Harbor. People from all over Baltimore were discovering how nice downtown was. The city was becoming more popular every year. Many young lovers came to the harbor to hold hands and stroll down the promenade in the evening and steal a kiss or two. Thousands of people came down to the Inner Harbor.

The Italian Festival was mobbed. The people who worked for me worked long hard hours in the heat of the summer. When Mayor Schaefer was determined to build the Aquarium he came to all the festivals to get people to sign his petition to have the Aquarium built. No one knew how big his idea was. People couldn't believe it would become the marvelous attraction it has become today.

The National Aquarium

The Mayor went on a trip to visit his friend Governor Dukakis of Boston, Massachusetts. Mr. Robert Embory and Mr. Rouse accompanied Mayor Schaefer on the trip. Mr. Rouse built the Aquarium at Faneuil Hall, in 1976. While Mayor Schaefer was in Boston, Governor Dukakis took Schaefer to visit the famous Market Place where their Aquarium is. Major Schaefer couldn't believe all the improvements that were made in Boston. He was especially impressed by the beautiful transformation that had taken place at the harbor.

Mr. Rouse was an excellent contractor and another friend of Mayor Schaefer. He also constructed the Aquarium in Boston. Mr. Rouse had created a new section of Maryland, known as Columbia. This new community is a thriving part of Maryland today.

When Mayor Schaefer saw all the people visiting the Aquarium in Boston, he became enchanted with it. He couldn't stop thinking about all the revenue it brought into the city. After Schaefer came back to Baltimore, he had the idea to build an Aquarium here.

Soon he started planning to make this possible. He received lots of negative response towards his idea. People called his project "Schaefer's Fish Bowl." He realized he needed a lot of help to persuade people to believe in his idea. He needed the big businesses in town on his side. The City Council, which my Uncle Dominic Mimi DiPietro was in, always voted with the Mayor. Mayor Schaefer believed the Aquarium would bring lots of people into Baltimore City.

Mayor Schaefer went to work to get people to believe in him. He eventually received help from the Blue Cross and Blue Shield, the Baltimore Gas and Electric Company, Whiting and Turner, Verizon, Mercantile Bank, and the Pantry Pride grocery store.

Mayor Schaefer was on a mission to change people's attitudes about Baltimore City. When he made his mind up to do something he was determined to make his project work. The mayor was a mover and a shaker. When he wanted something done, he wanted it done yesterday.

Mr. Bob Embory took a referendum before the Board of Elections to put a Bond issue to get the Aquarium built. After the referendum was put on the ballot the bill passed. Mr. Peter Charmayeff designed the Aquarium in the spring of 1977.

Mayor Schaefer and the Rubber Ducky

As the building progressed, the National Aquarium kept meeting hurdle after hurdle. Mayor Schaefer kept persevering through every obstacle. He made an resolution, if the National Aquarium was not built by a specific time, he would jump into the dolphin pool in an old fashioned swim suit with a rubber ducky. He wanted to show the public how committed he was towards this project.

He asked his friend Gene Raynor what he thought of this idea. Mr. Raynor replied, "Schaefer, I don't think this is such a good idea." When Mayor Schaefer jumped in the pool in his old time swim suit with a rubber duck, he received national attention. He made the cover of *Time* magazine, a national magazine. After this, Mayor Schaefer called Mr. Raynor and said, "The next time I want to ask you for some political advice, I will do the opposite of what you tell me to do."

The first year the National Aquarium opened, 18,000,000 visitors came to see it. Mayor Schaefer went on to make the National Aquarium the golden jewel of Baltimore, something he had set out to do all along. His love for Baltimore was seen in everything he did for his beloved city. Mayor Schaefer was the heart of Baltimore City. There will never be another like him. When Mayor Schaefer started to build up the Inner Harbor, people from all different states and countries came to visit the Inner Harbor every year. Today it is the number one major attraction for Baltimore City.

The Dollar Homes

Despite the fact Mayor Schaefer improved the Inner Harbor, he realized he had to do something to the neighborhoods surrounding it. He came up with another idea to improve the city he loved. There was going to be a high rise apartment building going up in South Baltimore overlooking the harbor. Mayor Schaefer didn't like this idea. He had other plans for the area. He presented a bond issue to put this matter to a vote. It was a good thing the bond issue did not pass.

In 1975 Mayor Schaefer got an idea from the Mayor of Wilmington, Delaware. The idea was to allow people of Baltimore to buy the homes for one dollar a piece. The homes were located around Otterbein Street. The terms of the agreement were for purchasing the homes for $1. The homes had to be restored to their originally magnificence.

A lottery was held in October, to let people bid on the homes. If more than one person bid on the same home, whoever won the lottery got the home. Mayor Schaefer made this a fun project. When I found out what Mayor Schaefer was doing, one of my construction worker friends took me to see the homes. We went inside the home he was remodeling. It was absolutely gorgeous. I wanted to buy a house there so bad because I loved the area. The water has always been where I wanted to live. When the sun shines on the water it creates a glossing affect. The sun makes the waves look like little stars in the water.

After I saw the entire home restored to its luster, it made me want to buy one of the homes there all the more. Everyone who bought one of the homes acquired the financing from the city. The stipulation was they had to fix the homes up to their original luster. There were one hundred thirteen homes in the Otterbein area. All the homes have been restored to their original luster. Phil Duby one of the customers from Sabatino's was one of the first persons to bid on one of the homes on Otterbein Street. Mr. Duby said after he won the bid on the home, Mayor

Richard Reische and Phil Duby, Sabatino regulars

Schaefer drove by and said, "Thank you and have a great time restoring the home."

Phil's brother Brian was an architect. He was the person who designed the reconstruction of the home Phil bought. Brian restored several homes in the area to their magnificent glory. It has been thirty four years since Mr. Duby bought one of these homes. He still lives there today.

While Mayor Schaefer was improving Baltimore City, I was working to improve my lifestyle, by having stands in the Baltimore City Fair, the Italian Festival, and the Fells Point Festival. Through these many festivals, I was able to buy my business on Belair Road in Baltimore. I called it Peachy and Boh's, Peachy for me and Boh for my father. I owned the business for ten years.

Chapter Five

Barbara Mikulski

Barbara Mikulski is a feisty Senator. She is the first Democratic woman ever to have served in both Houses of Congress. She is the first woman ever to win a statewide election in her home State of Maryland. She is blunt, outspoken, and feisty. She is a fierce debater. She planned to use her good mind and good mouth and good heart that God gave her to voice her opinion. Barbara is a staunch supporter of organized labor and wanted to save jobs.

Barbara was a granddaughter of Polish immigrants in Baltimore born on July 20, 1936. She inherited her can-do spirit and determination from her family. Both her grandfather and father were local shopkeepers. Her grandfather ran a bakery and her father had a grocery store. Mikulski helped out with her father's store in addition to studying hard in school. Her parents operated a grocery store called Willy's Market.

Barbara attended Catholic grade and high schools. She showed lots of talent when she was little. She coaxed her cousins and friends to take part in shows in her father's garage which she wrote, produced, and directed. Barbara aspired to be a scientist. When she saw a movie about French chemist and physicist Marie Curie the movie inspired her to be a chemist.

She wanted to be a nun but she was too rebellious. She trained to be a social worker. She studied at the University of Maryland and graduated in 1965 with a Master's degree in Social work. She is a fighter and never voted on popular issues. She was a street organizer. You could never describe her as mellow. When she walks in a room you definitely can feel her presence. She certainly was a liberal. Mikulski learned the values of hard work, neighbor helping neighbor, and heartfelt patriotism.

She started in politics in 1968 when she organized Baltimoreans from East Baltimore to block construction of a sixteen lane highway. It would

Governor Howard Hughes, Barbara Mikulski, Council Member Dominic Di Pietro, Mayor Thomas D'Alesandro in front of the statue of Christopher Columbus at the Inner Harbor

have destroyed East Baltimore including Historical Fells Point. Despite the opposition, Mikulski blocked the highway proposal. After she initiated this fight, she brought the neighborhoods together because of how she stopped the highway project. Her coalition, known as Southeast Council Against the Road, or SCAR, won their battle with City Hall.

By 1966 she was an assistant chief of community organizing for City Social Services Department. She worked primarily in cases of child abuse and neglect. She had a deep concern for the rights of children and families. Mikulski was the defender of immigrants who came to America. These were the people who constructed skyscrapers, operated the railroads, worked on the docks, fortresses, steel mills, and in the mines. They were ridiculed because of their language and culture of food. They formed an alliance on mutual issues, interdependence and respect.

This is what led her to run for a seat on the Baltimore City Council. In doing this she wore out five pairs of shoes knocking on 15,000 doors to spread the message throughout Highlandtown. She worked for five years in the City Council along with my Uncle Dominic (Mimi) Di Pietro. She was known to get things done along with my uncle. Between the two of them, they fixed anything and everything that was wrong with East Baltimore.

When Congressman Sarbanes ran for a Senate seat she ran to take his office. She became the first woman working on the Merchant Marine & Fisheries Committee and House Energy & Commerce Committee. It gave her the platform to lobby on railroads telecommunications and health care. She was an advocate for legislation to protect children and supported the Equal Rights Amendment.

After five years as congresswoman, in 1986 Mikulski set her sights on the U.S. Senate after Senator McMathias retired. Her opponent was Linda Chavez. Linda made people believe Mikulski was not qualified to be in the Senate because of her loud, rude, and frumpy looks.

Mikulski hired Lillian Brown to make her appear more attractive. She changed her glasses, dresses, and she learned how to sit properly. She also took advantage of camera advantages. She lost forty pounds by dieting and exercise. She also toned her East Baltimore language. She had the support from celebrities as singer Carly Simon and renowned feminist Gloria Steinem. They helped her raise the necessary funds for her successful campaign. She endured jokes at her expense about her preference for pants. After she became a strong advocate for her constituents, she earned their respect.

When she got in the Senate and sat in Harry Truman's old seat, she became a major player in the Senate. With the help of Senators Sarbanes and Byrd, they helped her land a job of Senate Appropriations Committee. She also served on numerous sub-

Me and Senator Barbara Mikulski

committees. She worked to help Maryland's Eastern Shore oyster beds. She knew she was going to make certain choices and they were going to be tough.

Barbara Mikulski is the longest serving woman Senator. She worked on behalf of women's issues, including legislation to get breast and cervical cancer screenings and treatment for the uninsured. For the elderly, Mikulski authored the Spousal Anti-Impoverishment Act. She combated the potential financial crisis caused by the costs of paying for nursing home care for a spouse. She supported and encouraged innovation and research in many areas as the chairwoman for the Subcommittee on Commerce, Justice and Science.

In weeks leading up to the Democratic National Convention she gave a speech stating this would be an historic election. It had more Democratic women running for Senate at one time than ever before. She said, "We have a tremendous opportunity to elect women and hold the Senate for Democrats. Women make a difference when we vote and when we lead."

In 2015, Mikulski announced she would be retiring. In response to hanging it up after 30 years of service rather than preparing for another re-election campaign, she responded in her typical blunt manner, "Do I spend my time raising more money, or do I spend my time raising hell?" Later that year, the longtime senator was honored as a recipient of the Presidential Medal of Freedom.

CHAPTER SIX

MY NEIGHBORHOOD

The History of Our Lady of Pompei

Let me tell you a story about my church. Our Lady of Pompei has been the icon of Highlandtown for decades. The church is the rock of the community and it has always upheld the well being of the community. The parishioners held the church to higher standards. There were strong neighbors who kept this neighborhood together for many years. Most of these people had businesses in the Highlandtown area.

This Church, my church, "Our Lady of Pompei", has been the main source of keeping the neighborhood together since 1924. Through their guidance and leadership they have kept the neighborhood strong. My Parish helped to instill in my life my religious beliefs.

After spending 17 years of missionary work in the land of China, Fr. Luigi Scialdone, C.M. came to Baltimore. He was from the Neapolitan Province of the Vincentian Fathers located in Naples, Italy. This was the same Province my Mom's family was from. The archbishop at the time, Michael J. Curley, appointed Fr. Scialdone to be the pastor and shepherd of the scattered Italian flock who were neglected immigrants. The Archbishop helped the Italian people of Highlandtown when he did this.

In the 1920's the world was full of hope. This is when the world of Our Lady of Pompei was born. While work was underway on the church, the community gathered to celebrate mass with Fr. Scialdone in the basement of the Sacred Heart Parish on Conkling Street. The Parish quickly became known throughout Highlandtown as "Pompei." The church was officially opened in June of 1924 at the 10 o'clock mass. The church was dedicated to the Blessed Mother under the title of "Our Lady of the Holy Rosary of Pompei." The people were yearning for security, comfort, and belonging. Our Lady of Pompei provided this for them.

In the twenties, many people enjoyed their business transactions and investments until the Stock Market Crash on Thursday, October 24, 1929. After this the immigrants were pushed further and further out of the mainstream. While this was going on Fr. Scialdone helped keep the neighborhood together.

Procession for the Blessed Mother

To commemorate the wonderful anniversary of the church there is a huge procession to honor the Blessed Mother. It is held every first Sunday in October. The event starts with a band playing music early in the morning. The band begins playing at Claremont Street where one of the band members, Mr. Mike Di Martino, lived. They marched to the corner of Conkling and Claremont Streets to the church.

The Knights of Columbus dressed in their wonderful attire escorted the statue of the Blessed Mother out of the church. My father, Carmen DiPietro, and his cousin, John Tana, were members of the Holy Name Society. They carried the statue of the Blessed

Procession for the Blessed Mother at Our Lady of Pompei

Mother on their shoulders. Many of the other men from the Holy Name Society also helped to carry the statute.

The procession started at Conkling and Claremont Streets. They marched through Highlandtown, and then returned to the church. The Knights of Columbus escorted the statue of the Blessed Mother back into church. The celebration of the Mass then took place.

As a child, I participated in the procession to honor the Blessed Mother. My sister Rosie and brothers Vince & John who were altar boys also participated in the procession. I wore my first Holy Communion dress along with all the children in my class. My cousin Clara along with all her sisters and brothers were also in the procession. The girls were dressed in their white communion dresses. The boys were in their white suits.

While the procession was going on, all the people in the neighborhood came out of their homes to show homage to the Blessed Mother. The whole neighborhood supported the church because they understood the importance of having the church in their neighborhood.

Some of the people who walked in the procession were: The Holy Name Society which was formed by Luigi Aiello. The Ladies of Charity was formed by Mrs. Carrie Bucher. Our Lady of Mount Carmel Society was formed by my grandmother, Anna DiPietro. My mother and aunts belonged to this society also. The boys and girls scouts formed by my aunt Ann Varner, which my children belonged to, also walked in the procession.

One year Cardinal Keeler, the acting Cardinal participated in the procession and attended the commemoration of the Mass. After the Mass the priest distributed fresh roses (the sign of the Blessed Mother) to the parishioners. Then everyone went to the School Hall where there was food, drink, music, and games for the people to enjoy.

The Priests of Our Lady Of Pompei

When Father Tomaselli became the pastor, he was the main person who wanted to build a new school. He had a slogan to get people interested in supporting the school. It read like this, "Search your heart, and do your part." All the school children went around the neighborhood to sell bricks to help build the school for fifty cents.

Many days my cousin Clara, friend Merle, and I went door to door to sell bricks to help build our new school. This was difficult to do. We would go outside our neighborhood. The people who lived in different parishes did not want to give to our church. They had their own church to support. Our neighborhood consisted of all working class people. They had to take care of their own families and church.

Fr. Tomaselli was the main person who was responsible for the building of Our Lady of Pompei High School. The school opened in 1959, and my children and my brother John attended it.

Some of the early priests who ministered their services at Our Lady of Pompei were Fr. Spiriti, Fr. Turturro, Fr. Hogan, and Fr. Mason. Fr. Petti came from Italy to Pompei. When Fr. Tomaselli retired, Fr. Petti became the pastor of my church. There also was Fr. Fiorentino, Fr. Noonan, Fr. Trotta, Fr. Cesa, Fr. Vadaaca, and Fr. Esposito.

Father Petti

When Fr. Petti came to Pompei from Italy my grandmother Annarella took him all through the neighborhood. She introduced him to all the parishioners. My Grandmother Annarella was involved with Our Lady of Pompei church constantly. She is the single person who instilled in her children and grand children to become involved in all of the church functions.

Father Petti was the priest who gave me the nickname Peachy. One morning after singing in the church choir we were all gathered outside of church talking. Father Petti came up to us and talked to us. He turned towards me and pinched my cheeks. He said, "You have 'Peachy' cheeks," in his heavy Italian accent. When my family heard this name, it stuck with me forever. Years later Fr. Fiorentino, Fr. Lou Esposito came to my parish. They were my children's teachers. Fr. Noonan, and Fr. Louis Trotta, (whose family lived in Highlandtown), are some of the priests who ministered their services at Our Lady of Pompei.

Father Lou Esposito & Father Lou Trotta

Father Lou Esposito is the Pastor of Our Lady of Pompei today. He came to Baltimore in 1964 at the young age of twenty four. When he came to Pompei he was the first young priest the children of the parish knew. The little children followed him around the neighborhood. He was

Fr. Lou Trotta and Fr. Lou Esposito at Our Lady of Pompei

a priest the children could relate to. They could not get enough of him. They loved him because of his fantastic personality. Most of the children are still friends with him today.

He bestowed kindness to them when they were young. They never forgot his kindness. My children were included in Fr. Lou's many teachings. The children of the Parish grew close to Father Lou Esposito. He talked to the children on their level. They appreciated all the attention he gave them.

Father Lou Trotta was considered the original "Peck's bad boy" of the neighborhood. He did several dumb things when he was young. He was always getting into fights and causing a lot of hardship for his family.

Father Scialdone told Father Lou Trotta, he would never make it as a priest. After this, Father Lou Trotta was determined to become a priest. He proved all those people wrong because in June of 2013, he was a priest for sixty-one years.

When Father Lou Trotta came back to Baltimore to visit his family during the Christmas and Easter holidays, the two Father Lou's became best friends. The two priests would go down to Patterson Park and play tennis together there. When the children in the neighborhood found this out they followed them down the park to watch them play. Sometimes the children played tennis with them also. The children loved to see them kidding and teasing one another. They were a big comedy show. This kept the children occupied and brought the children close to God and the church. When the children came to church their parents came with them. The two Father Lou's teased each other all the time which made everyone love them even more. They addressed themselves as Father Lou number one and Father Lou number two. When they gave sermons at church they made all the parishioners laugh because of all the funny stories they told about each other. Many of the parishioners couldn't wait until Father Lou Trotta came home on the holidays. They wanted to hear the two priests kid each other. They were great together. They told funny stories about one another making everyone laugh.

The Saint Lucy Fillipini Nuns

The school had the Fillipini Nuns from New Jersey. They taught the students of Our Lady of Pompei. They came to Highlandtown on August 27, 1928 upon the request of Fr. Scialdone. The first graduating class at Our Lady of Pompei had seven graduates, it took place on June 21, 1929.

The Nuns of Saint Lucy Fillipini educated most of the children from Highlandtown. All my siblings, cousins, and neighbor's children went to school there. The nuns instilled in the students great values for their family and faith. Because of the nuns, many of the students became involved in everything the school and the church did. The lessons taught to the children were of a higher level because of the nuns. The encouragement from the nuns and priests helped the children became responsible individuals. Most of the children went on to become prominent citizens and pillars of Baltimore and beyond.

The nuns knew if they kept the children involved in school projects they wouldn't get mixed up in bad activities. The nuns made the children perform in plays at school. My daughters, Anna and Michelle, were involved in many of the activities at the church.

On the cover of my first book you see me dressed as little Bo Peep. The nuns made me participate in the school plays. Another time I portrayed Saint Bernadette who saw a vision of the Blessed Mother. When I was on stage, I had to wash my face in dirt to find the holy water. Many pilgrims make the trip to Lourdes today to bathe in the special water there.

Some of the Supporters of the Church

The Altar of Our Lady of Pompei, my parish Church in Highlandtown

One of the early supporters of the church was Luigi Aiello who lived down the street from my grandparents. My grandmother Annrella Di Pietro, Luigi Di Pasquale from Di Pasquale's grocery store, and Luisa Castelazzi formed the Children of Mary which I belonged to along with my sister and cousins.

Alfred Santoni from Santoni's grocery store created the Holy Name Society. Pasquale Celozzi from Celozzi's grocery store formed Our Lady of Grace Society.

Joseph & Guy Ercole both helped to build the church brick by brick because they were brick layers. The church was everything to them. They put their church on the highest pedestal. The church was the root of Highlandtown. Many of these people helped form the church and make it what it is today. They contributed their own money and helped build the church brick by brick.

Mary Ercole cooked for the priests at Pompei along with M's. Christine. Both of these ladies cooked for the priests for many years.

There was the Mothers Club, which all the mothers of the children who went to school at Our Lady of Pompei belonged to, my Mom included. The mothers cleaned the church. They also brought their children to help clean it.

The people in the neighborhood always took care of the church. They were glad to help. They believed it was a pleasure to do this. Dr. John Constantini was also a generous contributor to the church. He always helped Fr. Petti. He gave the church many donations. He was always by Fr. Petti's side helping the church in whatever they needed.

The Di Pasquale's

Luigi Di Pasquale was the original owner of Di Pasquale's grocery store. He was one of the co-founders and a main investor of the Church. He helped to organize the beginning of Our Lady of Pompei.

Lou Di Pasquale helped supply food to the church when they had carnivals in the summer. Lou was close friends with Fr. Petti. He was the pastor of Our Lady of Pompei for many years.

All of the Di Pasquale children attended Pompei School. Most of the people who lived in Highlandtown were hard working people and they all sent their children to Our Lady of Pompei School. The church is the rock of the community. It has always cared about the well being of its parishioners.

There is a business in East Baltimore, Highlandtown to be exact, called Di Pasquale's. I bought all the Italian supplies from them when I had stands in the festivals and my sub shop. They have authentic Italian food. They always treated me kindly.

Their business started in 1914 on Claremont and Dean Streets by Luigi Di Pasquale, Sr. Mr. Lou Di Pasquale, one of Luigi's sons. He was born in America but Luigi was born in Abruzzi, Italy. This was the same town my grandparents Di Pietro's were from. When my grandparents came over on the boat to America from Italy, one of the Di Pasquale children helped my Grandmother. He watched her son Dominic Mimi Di Pietro. She was pregnant with my father Carmen at the time. All the movement on the boat made her sick through the entire trip to America. All the immigrants were kept in the bottom of the ship. The people who worked on the ship felt sorry for my grandmother. They allowed her to come above deck to get some fresh air.

All of the Luigi Di Pasquale children were born upstairs from the store in Highlandtown. When Luigi Di Pasquale, Sr. became sick in 1958, Lou Di Pasquale, Jr. was called by his mother to help in the local business. Luigi passed away in 1959 which left Lou Jr. to run the business.

After being at the same location for several years the Di Pasquale's moved their business to Gough and Dean Streets in 1988. It was a bigger location and they had more room to store the supplies they sold in the store. They also ran a wholesale business. In 2008 Guy Fieri from Dinners Drive-ins and Dives came to their store to interview Joe and Sabrina. Joe, Sabrina, and Joe's two sisters Anna Marie and Angela, run the business today. Joe and Sabrina showed Guy how they made their homemade pasta, sauce, mozzarella balls, rice balls, Lasagna noodles, and Lasagna. Guy stayed there for six hours interviewing them. Three years later he came back and did another segment on their business which was aired again on his show. The Di Pasquale's have just celebrated being in business for 100 years.

The Santoni's

The Santoni's were also strong supporters of the church. Yolanda and Savino Santoni were born in Italy and came to Baltimore in the 1900's.

Yolanda was born in Preverno, Italy and came to America in 1914 at six years old. Savino was born in Camerino, Italy and came to America in 1919 he was seventeen years old. After they met and fell in love, Yolanda and Savino got married in June of 1931.

Savino Santoni started his grocery store in the back of their home located at 119 S. Eaton Street. During this time there was a locally owned grocery store on every corner in Highlandtown. The Santoni's incorporated 111 to 119 S. Eaton Street to become their store. The homes used to be an old bar and a bowling alley. The customers were allowed to have charge accounts at the store. The Santoni's closed their store every Wednesday for a half a day. Many times a knock would come at their door. A customer would come to their home and ask if they could get what they needed. Naturally their son Bobby Santoni was elected to go the store for the customer.

After being located from 1944 to 1976 on Eaton Street, they moved their store to the corner of S. Eaton Street and E. Lombard Street. They bought the property across the street in 1987 at the 3800 block of Lombard Street in Highlandtown. This establishment now houses a larger and newer grocery store with a huge parking lot. They had a fantastic deli, with fresh produce, a bakery, and fresh meats and poultry displayed there. Altogether the Santoni's have been in business for eighty-two years.

All of the Santoni children went to Our Lady of Pompei Church and school; they were all baptized, and married here. Yolanda and Savino were buried from the church. Yolanda and Savino donated lots of their own money to the Church. They also donated money to the fund for the new school. The new school was built in 1955 on the corner of Conkling and Pratt Streets.

Most of the parishioners who lived in Highlandtown also contributed to the building of the new school. The school opened its first class in 1957. Most of the children from Highlandtown attended the school including my two children.

Louis Santoni went to school with my brother Vincent. Bobby Santoni attended school with my brother Johnny. Bobby Santoni would come to my home and work on special projects with my brother Johnny right on our kitchen table. Both of them became actively involved in making many projects together for school. I can remember watching them putting their heads together to accomplish what the nuns asked them to do. They worked for hours and because of this they became friends. The nuns were constantly giving the children projects to keep them busy and keep their minds occupied.

Sadly to say that after all the years the Santoni's have been in business they closed their doors for good in 2013. They had been in business for eighty three years.

Chapter Seven

My Love For Baseball

Baseball is one of the true loves in my life. My father's enthusiasm for the sport helped me to love the game as much as he did. My father played softball when he was a young man. He instilled in all of his children's hearts to love the game also. When my father was older he spent many hours in the evening after dinner listening to the ball game. He would sit out front of our home in the heat of the summer with his portable radio. Before evenings end my Mom and several of the neighbors joined him while he was listening to the game.

My father went to many Oriole games. He often took my brother Johnny with him. My father's brother, Mimi DiPietro was City Councilman for many years. He also was an ardent Oriole fan. He gave my father his passes to see several Oriole games.

When the O's played away he watched them on TV. My Mom wanted to go for a Sunday drive, because she had been working in the home all week. We all watched the O's play with my father. His enthusiasm for the game was the beginning of my love affair with the Orioles. After my children were born, I wanted them to love the sport the way I did. I took them too many Oriole games also.

Chuck Thompson

Chuck Thompson covered the games for the Baltimore Orioles on the radio. He broadcasted all the sports on the radio. His enthusiasm for all sports got you involved in whatever he was talking about. One day while driving in the car, he came on the radio talking about the Orioles. He said, "Bring your children to the stadium to watch the Orioles play. It's the cheapest entertainment in town. You will have a great time." When I heard this, I thought I would love to do this on my days off. I took the children to the ball park to watch the O's play. From then on my children and I went to many games the O's played on Monday and Tuesday evenings because they were my days off.

Jerry Turner

While you were waiting for the Orioles to come home from spring training, you could smell April in January. You lived for spring training. Jerry Turner was the famous news caster at WJZ TV. He talked about spring training all the time. He made everyone excited about opening day at Memorial Stadium. His enthusiasm about baseball made you love the game as much as he did. He worked at WJZ TV from 1962 as the lead anchor until his death in 1987.

Opening day was an event. People could hardly wait for it to come. All people thought about on this day was going to the ballpark. We had all the great players then; Brooks Robinson, Frank Robinson, Jim Palmer, Boog Powell, and Davy Johnson. We also had the best manager Earl Weaver. Everyone wanted to see these great players perform. Nobody wanted to go to school or work that day. Everyone took off to go to opening game. Memorial Stadium was full of energy; it was the place where legends were born and made.

The Hoffberger family

When the Hoffberger family owned the O's they also owned the National Brewing Company. The beer known as Natty Boh is on a comeback today. The enthusiasm of Patrick (Scunny) McCusker has featured the beer in his restaurant Nacho Mamas. Scunny said he was bringing Natty Boh back to the people whose grandfathers drank it before. My father was one of them.

After Mr. Hoffberger sold his Brewing Company, it left him with little incentive to own the Orioles. He sold his share of the Orioles to Mr. Edward Bennett Williams in 1979. He was a lawyer from Washington D.C. When he bought the Orioles everyone thought he would move them to Washington D.C. Mayor Schaefer was very concerned especially after losing the Baltimore Colts. He certainly didn't want to lose the Orioles also. When Mr. Bennett and Mayor Schaefer met, they both wanted to build a new ball park.

When Mayor Schaefer became Governor he was at a better position to deliver a new stadium for the people of Baltimore. The area they picked was an old railroad depot in the warehouse district in Baltimore.

The first game at the new stadium in Oriole Park at Camden Yards seated 47,000 people. The stadium was filled to

Maybe the most definitive brand of the city since 1885. While not brewed here anymore, about 90% of all of its sales are made in Charm City.

capacity during every game. Everyone from Baltimore and Washington came to see the O's play. Washington didn't have a team at this time.

After the Jacobs filed for bankruptcy, Attorney Peter Angelos and Cincinnati oil executive William Witt, became the new owners of the Baltimore Orioles. Mr. Witt's father once owned the Browns, the team we now called the Orioles. These two men are the majority owners of the Orioles. There are several other people who own part of the Orioles today also.

Going to the Ball Park

Through the help of several people, they helped me take my children to the ballpark many times. The people who helped me get tickets were Uncle Mimi Di Pietro, and my friends Warren Sollod and John Angelos.

Warren use to be a bat boy and this is where his love for the game started. He was working as a bat boy when the O's played the Yankees on September 20, 1958. Hoyt Wilhelm was the pitcher then and he pitched a no hitter against the Yankees. It was the first no hitter in Baltimore history.

People at the Stadium: Clancy

There was a man named Clancy who sold beer at the stadium on the first base side. Because we went to the stadium frequently Clancy always talked to us. He knew all the stats of the players, and he always talked about the players. He made everyone laugh because of the way he described the players, the umpires, and the game. He had a fantastic personality and all the fans loved him. When regular customers came to the game he would let them run a tab till the end of the game. Sallie & Jerry Trout were two of those people.

Wild Bill Hagey

We had one of the best fans ever. He was just an ordinary guy, a cab driver. When young people went to the ball park to see the O's, he created enthusiasm about the game. His named was Wild Bill Hagey. With his beard and belly which held a few adult beverages, he was easily recognizable. He only wore a T-shirt and jeans. What he did for the fans in Baltimore could never be matched ever again. He got all the fans to stand up and cheer for the O's. He acted out the word O-R-I-O-L-E-S with his body and everyone in the stadium did exactly what he did. He was one of the main reasons why young people came to the game.

Hillary and Larry Hammerman said, "He got all the young people involved in the game." On a special night of the week there would be three buck night at the stadium. All the young people wanted to sit in Wild Bill Hagey's section. His section was section #34, and everyone wanted to be able to cheer with him. He always brought the crowd to a roar. He excited the crowd so much and made everyone at the stadium have a great time. He especially made it cool for young girls to go to the ball park.

I interviewed people who went to the stadium and sat in Wild Bill's section. Here are some of the things they told me.

Morty Marcus said, "Wild Bill was the secret ingredient that made the Orioles popular in ways they weren't ever before. Wild Bill showed people it was okay to express your enthusiasm."

Dan Leibfeld said, "Wild Bill brought excitement to the game when sometimes it could become dull. He made everyone get involved in the team they loved."

Michael Olesker said, "One time the O's needed the crowd to roar. Rick Dempsey was in the dugout. He waved a white towel towards Wild Bill for him to start his cheer." Mike said, "Another night it started to rain and the crowd kept saying make it stop Wild Bill, make it stop." Wild Bill got up and waved his hat around as to scoop up the rain, guess what, the rain stopped.

It was a wild and crazy time then just like now. The O's were winning and everyone who came to the stadium cheered and had a great time. The O's were great and they are again now. Wild Bill Hagey brought such enthusiasm to the stadium you couldn't help but join in with his cheers. Wild Bill Hagey was the unofficial official cheerleader of the O's.

Rex Barney

Rex Barney was another great Baltimore announcer. He had a radio talk show on WBAL. He became the public address announcer for the Orioles at the stadium. I heard his wonderful voice many times. Every time a fan caught a foul ball Rex would say, "Give that fan a contract." Then he would say "Thank you" to the fan who caught the ball.

Before Rex Barney came to Baltimore he was a pitcher for the Brooklyn Dodgers. One time while he was pitching for the Dodgers, he struck out Joe DiMaggio. This was one of the most exciting games he played during his baseball career. He regretted his failure to have longevity as a MLB pitcher. Rex would come into Sabatino's after the ball games, with his friend Malinda Davis. I waited on these two wonderful people many times.

Because my children and I went to the ballpark often I met so many nice people. I had such great seats right down in front on first base side. Because of the great seats I had, one of the photographers from the *Baltimore Sun* paper took a picture of me cheering the O's to victory.

I met John, Lou, and Peter Angelos at Sabatino's. They are the main owners of the O's today. One time while waiting on Peter Angelos I asked him when he was going to get pitchers. He said, "I believe we have them young lady".

Some Great Players at Memorial Stadium:
Lee May

My daughter Michelle and I were at the ball park one evening. During the ninth inning the bases were loaded with two outs, Lee May came up at bat. He had two strikes on him. When the next pitch came, he hit the ball and it went all the way up and out of the stadium. It was a grand slam homerun on the last pitch in the ninth inning with two men out. The stadium went wild.

John Lowenstein

We were also at the stadium the night John Lowenstein stole home plate. We were there the night he caught a ball in the outfield and went right through the left field fence. He was an excellent clutch hitter. He formed a team with Gary Roenicke to form one of the most successful platoons in history together. In 1983 the pair combined to hit 34 home runs and drove in 124 runs.

Mark Belanger

My children and I were also at the stadium the night Mark Belanger hit a home run against the Yankees. The O's won the game and the stadium went wild. The way the fans reacted to this homerun you might have thought the O's won the World Series. There has always been such a rivalry between the Yankees and the O's and anytime we beat them it is a huge milestone. Besides the homerun in April 19, 1974, he also hit one on May 25, 1981.

One evening the O's were playing the Chicago White Sox and the O's had the lead 6-2. It was a cold miserable day and in the late innings the White Sox started to come back. They had a runner on first and someone hit the ball in the gap in left field. The runner could have easily scored.

Me and Earl Weaver at Sabatino's

Mark went into the outfield to take the cut off throw. The throw he made to the plate went all the way from the outfield to the catcher. Mark was the only guy who could make that play. The runner was out at the plate. Earl said, "Mark was one of the greatest defensive shortstops he ever saw."

Earl Weaver

Earl Weaver was one of the best managers anyone could have. He inspired all the players to do better. He managed the Orioles from 1968 to 1986. He often came into Sabatino's after the games, were I waited on him. When the Orioles played on the weekends he brought his family in with him.

He said there were three main purposes of spring training:

1) the players need to condition their bodies and mind for the grind to a 162 game series.

2) I have to use the workouts and games to pick my 25 man roster.

3) The veteran players need to review fundamentals. The new comers have to learn my style of playing the game. Earl said he never worried about winning in spring training. He spent his time looking at the players.

Earl had ten laws: 1) No one's going to give a damn in July if you lose a game in March. 2) If you don't make any promises to your players, you won't have to break them. 3) The easiest way around the bases is with one swing of the bat. 4) Your most precious possessions on offense are your 27 outs. 5) If you play for one run, that's all you'll get. 6) Don't play for one run unless you know one run will win a ball game. 7) It's easier to find four good starters than five. 8) The best place for a rookie pitcher is long relief. 9) The key step for an infielder is the first one to the left or right but before the ball is hit. 10) The job of arguing with the umpire belongs to the manager. It won't hurt the team if he gets thrown out.

Earl has been thrown out of the game by every one of the umpires. It was a total of 91 times. He said, "Don't curse the umpire curse the call." Earl always did what was good for the team. He taught the players the fundamentals to win games.

Earl taught all his players how to concentrate and execute the fundamental drills. He did this with enthusiasm and care every spring. They did it the same in their 10th year as they did in their first. They could do the fundamentals in their sleep and they never let him down. The guys who executed his drills were: Frank Robinson, Brooks Robinson, Jim Palmer, Eddie Murray, and Mark Belanger. Weaver broke in over 100 rookies, such as Murray, Dauer, Bobby Grech, Don Baylor and Al Bumbrey. They all started under him.

Jim Palmer

Me and Jim Palmer at Sabatino's

They hardly ever needed a relief pitcher when Jim Palmer started on the mound. He pitched the entire game. He was the master of all pitchers. He completed 211 games. Jim worked out the mechanics of his delivery. Palmer was ready when the bell rang. He was one of the best in the game. He is now in the Hall of Fame.

All summer long the sportswritr writers worried if Palmer would be ready. When it was time for him to go on the mound he was always ready. Jim had one of the most fluid motions the game has ever seen. If he appeared awkward, you knew something was wrong.

Jim Palmer was a three time CY young winner. He was on his way to having seven years of winning 21 games straight. He won these awards in 1970's, to 1978. In 1974 he missed eight weeks with his elbow problems. This was the only exception. Sometimes after the game was over, he would come into Sabatino's with his friends.

Interviewing People

I interviewed some of Sabatino's customers who have been Oriole fans for many years, here are some of their comments.

"When Jerry Hoffberger was the owner of the O's he would walk around the ball park to all the different sections and talk to the people."

Me and Rick Dempsey at Sabatino's

Ed Attman said, "Jerry Hoffberger was a very congenial man."

Stu Winestein said, "Rick Dempsey was a real Oriole. He belongs to the Orioles. He is an electrifying person. He motivated people, and brought excitement into the game." Stu said, "Rick bleeds orange. Rick's tenacity and his desire to compete rubbed off on his teammates. Rick's spirit was the biggest contribution to the O's team."

Warren Sollod said, "When there was a rain delay at the stadium Rick dressed up like the Babe. He stuffed pillows and towels in his uniform to make him look heavy like the Babe. He mimicked Babe Ruth when he went to the plate and pointed the bat to outfield. He then made out he hit a homerun. He made antics with his arms waving them in the air and waddle like a duck after he hit the ball. He did the same thing at each base and then he slid into home plate in the rain."

He was a natural born performer and oh how the fans loved him. Rick loved baseball and gave his heart and soul to the game putting everything in it. He wanted to win badly. Rick was a great defensive player. He had a terrific arm as a catcher. He threw out fifty-three percent of the runners in 1976. He threw out fifty-eight percent of the runners who tried to steal against him in 1977. He led the league in this. He had one of the best arms in the majors. He threw out 48% of runners in 1979

The day the Orioles won the 1983 World Championship President Reagan called the Orioles to congratulate them. He talked to Rick Dempsey who was the MVP of the game. This is what Rick told President Reagan. "Mr. President you go tell the Russians we're having an awful good time over here playing baseball." Rick Dempsey was the unlikely World Series MVP.

Dan Leibfeld and Mike David said, "Rick Dempsey was a bright spot on a dreary day."

Michael Olesker said, "He loved the entertainment Rick Dempsey brought to the sport. He always made it interesting. He was electrifying and he excited his teammates and the fans. Everyone loved him. While he did his special antics, he kept people at the ball park during the rain delay. He kept all the fans interested in the game".

Rick Dempsey came to the Orioles with a trade from the Yankee's in June 1976, along with Tippy Martinez, Rudy May, Dave Pagan, and Scott McGregor.

Some Great Orioles:
Eddie Murray

Eddie Murray came to Baltimore in a special trade in 1973. He was a third round pick. His first year in the majors was in 1977. He didn't have a chance of making the batting lineup. He hit his way to the top of the order. When Eddie Murray came to the Orioles, this was the beginning of the fabulous season known as Orioles Magic.

Eddie was always better when the game was on the line. When there was an important runner on second base Eddie became a better hitter.

Me and Terry Crowley, Mike Hargrove, and Eddie Murray at Sabatino's

Eddie batted three hundred when there was a man on base. When the score was 3-2 that's when he really did good.

Eddie won the first game of the double header by hitting a three run homerun in the bottom of the ninth to win the game 8 to 6. The O's came from behind to win

In June of '79 on a Friday night double header with Detroit, it was the bottom of the 9th. There were two men on and DeCences hit a home run. In the second game the O's were losing in the 8th inning. Eddie came up to bat and hit a home run and that was the start of Oriole's Magic in 1979. Terry Crowley pinch-hit in the bottom of the eighth inning. His single won the game.

Eddie put career numbers up in 1983 with 33 home runs 111 RBI's and a .306 average. He belted two home runs in the World Series game #5 clinching the victory.

Frank Robinson

Frank Robinson was traded to the Orioles on December 9, 1965 for Milt Pappas, Jack Balschun, and Dick Simpson. The owner of the Cincinnati Reds traded Frank Robinson. They considered Frank to be too old at the age of 30 to play. In 1966 he led the O's to the pennant and the World Series title, their first World Championship. Frank won the MVP award in 1966 and the Triple Crown. His batting average was 316. He hit 49 home runs and 122 RBI's in the same year while playing for the Orioles.

Previously he had won rookie of the year when he played for the Cincinnati Reds in 1956. He won MVP in 1961 when he played for them. He was the first and only player to win the MVP in both leagues. Frank was inducted into the Hall of Fame in 1982.

Frank became angry when the pitcher struck him out. He set his mind to hit the ball out of the park in the next at bat. If a guy made a great catch on Frank, he'd tell himself he would hit a ball so far no one would be able to catch it. It really bothered him when he got out. He knew he would succeed at the next opportunity. Frank realized a 9-2 lead in the seventh inning isn't always safe. Frank's concentration was fabulous. He frequently comes to Sabatino's. I have waited on him and his wife many times.

Brooks Robinson

When Brooks Robinson played baseball he played like he came from a higher league. He holds so many records it will take a very long time for anyone to ever approach them. Some of the awards he won were most career games played as a third baseman 2,870. Brooks had the most career assists as a third baseman 6,205. The second place person was Grieg Nettles who had 5,279. Brooks had the most career double plays by a third baseman 618. His most put outs by a third basemen was 2,697. He has the highest career fielding average, most career double plays, most years leading third base in fielding coverage, most hits by a third baseman in Baseball History.

His honor awards are 16 straight Gold Gloves since 1960 to 1975as the best third base defensive player. He was named to the American League all star team from 1960 to 1974. He won the outstanding professional Athlete award of 1970, the most Valuable player in the 1970 World Series. He also won the American League's Most Valuable Player in 1964.

Once Brooks was asked what his most memorable plays were, he said, "It was about the drives I pulled against the Reds in the 1970 World Series."When Doug DeCines took over Brooks Robinson's place at third base in 1977 he picked up third base and gave it to Brooks.

After they each hit back to back home runs in the first inning, on October 5, 1966 Frank and Brooks were affectionately known as the Robinson twins.

Don Drysdale was pitching for the Brooklyn Dodgers, then and the O's won 5 to 2. Years later when Don Drysdale became a Sports Announcer, he came into Sabatino's with his associates. I waited on all of them while they had dinner there. He was a very congenial person and signed many autographs that night.

Hillard Folus and Renee Sherman, great Oriole fans

Brooks Robinson had suffered a lot of hits by pitchers in his major league career. He was hit 53 times in his career. Since he started spring training it never dawned on him to stay loose. He stuck his head out there and dug in and swung the bat. Brooks said you need quick reflexes. You have to be willing to stick your chin out and let the ball bounce on your body.

When he was playing he would go out to the ball park earlier and earlier for batting practice. Brook's main objection was to stay in the best shape. He knew this was the only way he could stay in the majors and remain there.

You have to concentrate to play ball. He always said, "Concentration is vital." While he played third base, he could always tell when a player was going to bunt. He was always trying to master his throws.

Brooks said, "You have to know your players whether to play deep or not." He never took his eye off the ball.

Hillard Folus said, "When Brooks Robinson played third base, he stood ten to twelve feet behind it, he caught the ball with his glove. Then he threw the ball to first base and got the man out all the time. "The reason he was able to do this," Hillard said, "Was because he held his glove down low to the ground. He was able to pick the ball up fast and throw it to first base and get the guy out." Brooks was one of the fans favorite players and he was also the favorite of all the players. He was a down to earth person and this is why everybody loved him.

Cal Ripken Jr.

Cal Ripken Jr.'s values were instilled in him by his father Cal Ripken Sr. He told him to be honest and sincere in everything he did. He told him to work hard at anything he did. He also said anything you put your time and energy in you should do it with excellence. Cal always listened to his father who told him when you believe in something and you think is right you have to be strong enough to have the courage to stand up for it.

Cal's coaches were trying to decide whether to start him out as a pitcher or an infielder. Cal said, "I sure appreciate you asking Mr. Peters, but pitchers only play one out of five days. I want to play every day." This is how his career started.

Cal loved what he did and this is why he chose to break Lou Gehrig's record.   He thought it was great going to the ball park everyday to play. In his second full season as shortstop Cal established himself as a team leader batting .318 with 27 home runs and 102 RBI's. He was voted the 1983 American League MVP.

Cal would be the first shortstop in the history of the American league to win two MVP awards in a career. He had 30 home runs in one season and won the AL-MVP award in 1991. He won the Golden Glove in 1991 after missing out in 1990. He set the single season record for both fewest errors by a shortstop (3).

Boog Powell

Boog was much happier and played better when he could eat all he wanted. Earl suggested he lose weight because the GM told Earl to tell him this. He was the MVP in the American League in 1970, while weigh-

Boog Powell at his famous Barbeque stand at Camdem Yards

ing 270 lbs. He played in four World Series in 1966, 1969, 1970, and 1971.

In 1970 it was his best post season run. He has always been a big man but he always played well no matter how heavy he was. He now owns a restaurant at the new ball park called Boog's BBQ and one down in Ocean City, Maryland.

Al Bumbry

Al was the ideal leadoff hitter. He was the rookie of the year in 1973, when he was hitting .337. Earl liked to put the men up first who could always get on base. This is what Al Bumbry did all the time. He played a part in the 1979 loss to Pittsburgh. He was part of the Orioles in 1983 when they won the World Series and beat Philadelphia. During a very private part of his life, Al was a sergeant in the service. He was awarded a Bronze Star. He was the platoon leader in Vietnam before he became a baseball player.

Mike Flanagan

Mike was the heart of the O's pitching staff. On May 18th against the team he suffered a knee injury. Fans stood up and cheered. The left hander made his way from the bull pen to the field. The fan reaction made him feel good. It pumped him up more than he would have been. He was trying to stay relaxed.

He started the final game of the series against Texas on August 17, 1983. He hung tough allowing only 10 hits. He only allowed two runs through nine innings. This was enough for the O's to cling to a 2-2 tie. Then Mr. Clutch of 1983 Dan Ford delivered the game winning RBI double in the tenth, which gave the O's a 4 to 2 victory.

This was Flanagan's first win since May 11th giving him a 7-2 record. After this game Flanagan's left foot was bleeding because of the hard mound at Arlington Stadium. He never complained he kept pitching until the game was over.

Joe Altobelli

Joe Altobelli wasn't the first choice to replace the legendary Earl Weaver as manager at the start of the 1983 season. His laid back approach turned out to be exactly what the veteran ball club needed.

People said Baltimore was a "we"team and not an "I"team. There was no jealousy or animosity in the team only the desire to win a championship. Memorial Stadium was full of energy then, it was where legends were born and made.

After having all of these fabulous players and all the wonderful plays made by the Orioles this is why I loved them so. My father loved the game so he never missed a game.

A Comic Empire

After working many odd jobs in the neighborhood, there was a young man who worked at Sabatino's as a bus boy for many years. His name is Steve. He was a local boy who lived in Little Italy and knew everyone who lived in the neighborhood. When he got older, he became a mailman. He loved comic books so much that it consumed his whole conversation.

While he delivered the mail, he became friendly with his customers. He has such a fantastic personality he easily drew people into his conversations. You could not help but become engrossed in his enthusiasm. He started to talk to his customers about his comic book collection. Eventually, he started trading his comic books with his customers. Then he found out about places in Philadelphia he could go and sell his comic books.

He is a very strong willed person, and he believed he could do well trading his comic books. Eventually his comic book collection got so big he quit his great mailman's job and started trading his comic books for a living. He became so popular he eventually got a job for the Baltimore Magazine. Then later he became the editor of it.

He now owns the Baltimore Magazine, and has a huge comic book distribution company. He is also part owner of the Baltimore Orioles. He is a motivator for all young people who look up to him which they do today. He is one of the nicest people I know and his name is Steve Geppi.

Picture in the Paper

Because I went to the stadium to watch the Orioles' often, I had great seats right down in front on the first base side. A photographer for *The Sun Paper* took a picture of me cheering the Orioles on to a win and put it in the paper.

Every Friday evening Judge Jerome Robinson and district attorney Joe Murphy came into Sabatino's for dinner. The Judge asked me if I saw the picture they put of me in *The Sun Paper* cheering the Orioles to victory. I told him I hadn't seen it. He told me not to worry; he would get me a copy of the picture. The next week when the Judge and Joe came into the restaurant, the Judge brought the picture to me. The picture showed how much fun I was having cheering for the O's.

The Queen

On May 15, 1991 the Queen of England Queen Elizabeth and Prince Phillip came to Baltimore to watch the O's play. The game was against the Oakland A's and Oakland won 6 to 3. They were on a visit to Washington and after their visit, President George H.W. Bush and his wife Barbara escorted them to Baltimore. This was the first baseball game they had ever seen. She received a standing ovation from the fans, but they only stayed for two innings. This was the last year the O's played at Memorial Stadium. The next year the O's moved to Oriole Park at Camden Yards.

The Oriole Bird at the Ballpark

John Denver

My love for John Denver began when I saw the movie he made about Annie. Ever since then I have been in love with his music. It is so calm and relaxing I love it. Because I went to many games and whenever it was the 7th inning stretch they played "Thank God I'm A Country Boy." It has been a Baltimore O's tradition since the 1970's.

When John Denver came to Baltimore for a concert engagement, I was hoping he would come to the Ball Park to sing his famous song "Thank God I'm A Country Boy" and he did. I was working because it was a Saturday evening. He came to Camden Yard to sing and dance with the O's bird. They both danced to his famous song right on top of the O's dugout for the 7th inning stretch. The date was September 20, 1997 against the Detroit Tigers and the crowd went wild.

Once he left Baltimore he went home. He wanted to surprise his friend Clint Eastwood. Three weeks later as he was flying his plane over Monterey, California to Clint's home, his plane crashed into the water. He and his plane were scattered all over the water in small pieces. What a tragedy. It was a Sunday evening October 12, 1997. This was only three weeks after he left Baltimore.

The New Orioles and Buck Showalter

I have been going to the stadium for many years waiting to see the Orioles have another winning season. I always believed in them no matter what. With the help of Buck Showalter they have a great chance to make it to the playoffs and beyond. Buck has been the best manager we have had for some time. He has brought the team to where they are today. His unique technique has formed the team to perform to the best of their ability. He makes everyone Buck-Up.

There are so many good players today I believe they have the best chance to forge ahead and make it to the playoffs and beyond. With such players as Adam Jones who is the best outfielder we have had in some time. Then there is Matt Wieters who has a powerful arm as a catcher.

Chris Davis is coming back this year. With the number 19 how could he not be good? J.J. Hardy is another player you can count on. He gives his all when he comes up to bat or when he plays the infield. Jonathan Schoop, Nolan Reimold, and Ryan Flaherty they are hitting their way to a year of success.

Mark Trumbo became the first Oriole to hit two home runs in the same inning. He has been the homerun hitter for the Orioles this year. He has hit more homeruns in the league than any other hitter.

We are probably watching one of the best players in Manny Machado. He gives his all in everything he does. Whether he plays defense or is at bat we can always depend on him to do his best. I have been watching him for years. I even created a song for him "Oh Manny we love you."

Hyun Soo Kim did not start the year as a great contributor to the O's bullpen. He has worked harder to adjust to the pitches and speed. With the help of the hitting coach Scott Coolbaugh he has been doing much better.

We also have pitchers like Chris Tilman, and Daren O'Day, Kevin Gausman and they are pitching the O's toward a year of greatness. Zack Britton hasn't given up a run since April with his great pitching.

Tyler Wilson made the decision to pursue baseball even though he was an honor roll student with a degree in biology. After he got picked by the O's in the draft he knew which way to go. He wants to give the team a chance to win. His father Philip was also a pitcher. He has been coaching his son.

I believe they can go all the way this year. The players wearing the O's uniform today are playing more aggressively than they have in the past.

It is very ironic since they changed their sign back to the old BIRD they have been winning. I wonder if the old BIRD had anything to do with their winning again. I love my ORIOLES.

The National Aquarium at the Inner Harbor

Chapter Eight

The Circle One Restaurant

One of the most iconic restaurants I worked at was The Holiday Inn's roof top restaurant downtown in Baltimore on Howard Street. The Circle One Restaurant had the most fantastic view of the City of Baltimore. It was magnificent. This was way before the Inner Harbor was transformed into the beautiful show place it is today. The Hotel had a roof top restaurant that revolved while you were dinning. You would be able to see all the way across the Harbor as far south as Federal Hill and beyond. With the lights glistening on the water, it made it appear as if stars were shinning on the water. Besides the fabulous food and wonderful prices people came to see the panoramic view.

Becoming a Waitress

Because I was a single parent, I had to get a second job to support my children. When I went out into the working world, I met a woman who worked in a little sandwich shop. The shop was across the street from where I worked, Anderson Olds on Howard and 25th streets. Her name was Flo and she was exactly like the TV character Flo. She told me to become a waitress. She said once you become a waitress

Michelle and Anna

you will have enough money to take care of your children. With her advice I went to apply for a job as a waitress.

The restaurant I applied to served a five course dinner which included appetizer, soup, salad, main course, and dessert for a reasonable price. With this great value and the amount of food served, the restaurant was constantly busy.

The first night I worked at the restaurant, I followed one of the waitresses. She showed me where to go to pick up my drinks, food, and dessert. I thought to myself that it seemed easy until the following evening when I had to work by myself.

Michelle and Anna in front of my parent's home

The one thing I didn't realize was while I was working in a certain section, the restaurant revolved. After you left the station you were working in, the section kept moving.

The night I followed the waitress was a Thursday evening and everyone ordered French onion soup. The waitress told me to put croutons and cheese on top of the soup. The next evening was Friday. All the customers ordered clam chowder. Because of what the waitress showed me the other evening, I put croutons and cheese on everyone's clam chowder I served. I believed this was the restaurant's policy. My father always put cheese on his soup which led me to believe the restaurant did this to all of their soup. I thought to myself, wait until I tell my father what they do at the restaurant.

Later that evening, the last customers I waited on said to his wife, "Honey I thought we ordered clam chowder?" Replying to them, "Oh yes sir, it is clam chowder. We put croutons and cheese on the soup here." As I said this to the customer another waitress came by and said to me, "Leonora, we don't put croutons and cheese on clam chowder." All night long the other waitresses had been laughing at me. No one told me I was doing the wrong thing. Instead of helping me, they were all making fun of me the entire evening.

My parents, Carmen and Phyllis in front of their home

My first Saturday night working at the Holiday Inn was a disaster. I was taught to write the order on a duplicate pad and then rewrite it when I presented it to the customer. My duplicate pad was misplaced and I was beside myself. I hid in the linen closet, crying my eyes out, thinking to myself what a mess I made. How did I ever believe I could be a waitress? The manager went looking for me. One of the bus boys told him where I was. He asked me what the matter was. After telling him what happened, he said, "Don't worry, I will explain to the customer." He stayed with me all evening and taught me how to become a good waitress. Because of his help everything went well.

After this evening I tried to become a better waitress. I paid more attention to what I was doing. Taking care of my children became easier after I had the extra income coming in.

There was a man who worked in the kitchen and his job was to keep the kitchen floor clean. At the restaurant we wore white uniforms. While trying to serve the customers better, I took a short cut through the kitchen to get to the other side. The man was constantly mopping the floor. As I went into the kitchen, I slid all the way over to the ice-cream box on the other side. By the end of the evening, my white uniform was usually covered with everything I served all over it. After working at the restaurant for a while, the short cuts became easier for me.

At the Circle One restaurant, I met a wonderful woman named Jean and we became friends. She was a little older than I and she took me under her wing. She helped me become a better waitress.

Jean had two children. During the summer months she took me and my children along with her children on day trips to parks. Jean would say, "Come on lets go on a picnic." We'd pack a lunch and take the kids to some park, the Zoo, or the beach. We spent the day with our children having fun for little money. She was so good to me and my children and she helped me along the way in my life. Even though we weren't wealthy we both managed to have a good time with our children.

On one extremely busy Saturday evening, I loaded my tray with all the food that was needed to serve the customers. While the restaurant was revolving, I went into my station. When I went to put the tray on the stand, I misjudged it. All the food on the tray erupted all over me. There I was sitting in the middle of the dining room on the floor with lots of food all over me and my white uniform.

The restaurant had a violin player He played requests for the customers on the weekend. He didn't know what to do to help me, he was beside himself. He had never been in a situation like that before.

There also was a German waiter working with me. He came over to me and handed me one napkin. He said in his very German accent, "Here honey, wipe yourself off." This made me laugh and cry at the same time.

After cleaning myself off, I managed to finish serving my customers. This put me in the weeds big time. Even though I worked hard all evening I was never able to get caught up. Therefore it was an uneventful evening for me.

There was a beautiful garden on the balcony outside the restaurant. The customers could walk out there to get a better view of the City. One Sunday afternoon when I came to work, there were several police cars in front of the hotel. The Police made me enter the hotel from the back entrance. When I got inside, I learned the awful truth. A woman jumped to her death from the balcony. She went onto the balcony and hid there until the restaurant closed. Then she jumped off and landed on the awning below. After this horrible accident, the balcony was closed and no one was allowed out there again.

When the Beatles came to Baltimore they stayed at the Holiday Inn. They performed at the Civic Center which was across the street from the hotel. When the young girls found out the Beatles were staying at the Holiday Inn, they swarmed the hotel all evening. They were in the elevators and running all through the halls looking for the Beatles.

The next big star appearing at the Civic Center was Frank Sinatra. The restaurant was extremely busy that evening. People came in to dine at the restaurant before they went to see Frank sing. All I got to see of Frank Sinatra was his limousine leaving the side entrance of the Civic Center.

After a couple years of working at the restaurant, some of the other waitresses started talking about the new restaurant going to open in Towson. The restaurant was owned by the one and only Johnny Unitas and the defensive end Bobby Boyd. It was called The Golden Arm. The other waitresses said it was going to become a very popular place.

While I worked at the Circle One I also kept my day job. I could count on it to help pay some bills. My job at Anderson Olds was right down in the showroom. I was the secretary for all the sales men, the sales manager Mr. Kid and Mr. Mortimer. One day the sign from Johnny Unitas' Golden arm restaurant rode past the showroom window. When I saw the sign ride by, I believed it was a sign for me to go there and apply for a job. On my lunch break, I got one of the workers Bobby from the parts department to ride me to Unitas' to apply for the job.

When I entered the restaurant, there were several people sitting in the first both. They were the construction workers who were fixing the restaurant. One of them said, "She's pretty I would hire her." To my surprise I was hired. I was excited to get the job. It never occurred to me that I never had a car, not realizing I would have to take buses and cabs to get back and forth to work. The only thing that mattered to me was I was going to be working for Johnny U, the most fabulous player ever.

This was the beginning of a long relationship with some of the people I worked with. Some of the women who worked there were in the same situation as me. We were all supporting our children alone. Most of these women and I remain friends today. Of course there also was my love for the Baltimore Colts.

Vibrant businesses at the Inner Harbor

Chapter Nine

The Golden Arm

One of the most iconic persons in Baltimore was Johnny Unitas. Here is a story about his restaurant and his fate.

The restaurant was owned by the famous Baltimore Colt players, Johnny Unitas the quarterback and Bobby Boyd the cornerback. When I worked at the Golden Arm for several years it was the most wonderful experience of my life. I was able to meet many famous people that came into the restaurant while I worked there. One of the famous people was Carl Rosenblum the owner of the Baltimore Colts. When I met these people, they treated me as if I were their equal. This astonished me, the way they welcomed me. I was never in the presence of so many famous people at one time. It was exciting to be waiting on all the Baltimore Colt players and their wives. There were also many wonderful customers and movie stars who frequented the Golden Arm also.

John Unitas personified and represented professional football. He had the determination to lead the Baltimore Colts to many winning seasons. He led the Baltimore Colts to the NFL Championship in 1958 and 59 and also the Super Bowl in 1970. The Riots.

While I worked at Johnny Unitas' Golden Arm restaurant, the riots broke out over the City of Baltimore. The wonderful Rev. Martin Luther King had been shot in the month of April of 1968. Riots were going on in all the cities all over the United States. It was difficult for me or anyone who lived in the city to get to work, shop, or whatever people needed to do to survive. As you went out into the streets of Baltimore you had to pass through all the devastated areas where the riots were taking place.

One evening after the Baltimore Colts played the Green Bay Packers, the famous quarterback Bart Starr came into the restaurant. The Baltimore Colts had won the game on this day. Bart Starr sat at the piano and sang this song to Johnny U, "He's got the whole world in his hands, he's

Me in front of the Golden Arm

got the whole world in his hands." It was a wonderful evening, everyone was clapping and cheering. The customers couldn't believe what Bart Starr was doing. All the older football players were all friends. When Bart Starr sang this song to Johnny, he did this to honor him. He admired Johnny and it was a mutual friendship they had for each other. What a moving experience everyone had on this special evening.

When all the old players from the different teams came to Baltimore, they came into Johnny's restaurant. On another evening Jim Nabors came in and he sang at the piano also. The days I worked at the Golden Arm were so memorable to me and I will cherish them forever.

The Release of Johnny Unitas

Everyone who lived in Baltimore and knew Johnny Unitas loved him. He was a genuine, sincere, and humble person. If you lived in Baltimore during the time they traded Johnny Unitas to San Diego you were truly upset. How they traded Johnny was unconventional. People still talk about it today.

The owner of the Baltimore Colts, Carl Rosenblum told Johnny he would have a 10 year contract with the Colts when he stopped playing. He was going to be a consultant for the team after he retired. In fact, Johnny was supposed to have three choices of what he wanted to do for the Colts. Then Carl Rosenblum sold the Baltimore Colts to Bob Irsay. What they did actually was trade football teams.

One day when Johnny and his wife Sandy were leaving for Florida, Larry Harris a reporter for *The Baltimore Sun Paper* called him. He asked Johnny what he thought about the idea of going to San Diego. Johnny said, "I'm not going to San Diego, I'm leaving on a speaking engagement in Florida with my wife Sandy." Larry said, "Oh yes Johnny you are going to San Diego, you have been traded to them." This is how Johnny Unitas found out his fate.

Joe Thomas was the General Manager of the Baltimore Colts after Bob Irsay bought the team. Joe fired Coach Mac Cafferty after the Colts had four straight losses. He named John Sandusky be the interim coach. He was the assistant coach at the time. Joe Thomas told Sandusky not to play Unitas even though Thomas knew Sandusky and Unitas were friends. John Sandusky told Johnny Unitas what Joe Thomas told him. Unitas said, "It is their team and they can do whatever they want."

Subsequently after the sports writer from *The Sun Paper* told Johnny he was going to be traded, Johnny knew he wasn't going to stay in Baltimore much longer. Ernie Accorsi was the Public Relations man for the Baltimore Colts. He called Johnny and told him Joe Thomas wanted to

Johnny Unitas leaving the field at Memorial Stadium

talk to him. Joe Thomas told Johnny U he had been traded to San Diego. Johnny asked Joe what happened to the 10 year contract I was supposed to have with the Colts. He told Joe he was supposed to work in the office as a consultant. Joe told Johnny there was no stipulation in the contract about him staying in Baltimore.

After Carl Rosenblum mysteriously drowned in Florida in the water behind his home, Johnny had no proof of his conversation with Mr. Rosenblum. Rosenblum was considered an excellent swimmer. He won many championships for swimming when he was young. There is still an array of mystery about how such an ardent swimmer could drown this way. Later after Rosenblum drowned one man suddenly rose out of the water in a wet suit. It was very strange no one investigated the drowning of Rosenblum or what took place after this incident.

In the long and short of the situation, Johnny was screwed. Johnny had no other choose but to go to San Diego. Once Rosenblum passed away, his wife Georgia Frontiere, who previously was a stripper on the block in Baltimore, before marring him, now owned the Saint Louis Rams. Later she moved the Rams from Los Angeles to Saint Louis and took the name and the colors with her. After this she forced Carl's son Steve, who was an executive in the organization, out of the team.

Here is the best part; Johnny told his wife Sandy, we are going to San Diego. Johnny said, "Sandy they gave me the biggest contract I ever received playing football. He said, "The contract was for $250,000. That was the most money Johnny ever received during his entire career".

Johnny U was extremely disappointed at the way the whole situation was handled. Sandy said, "Johnny was deeply hurt." He was also disappointed in how the NFL treated the older players. Since Roger Goodell became commissioner, he has been working with the players to make changes come for the older players.

Johnny U's last Days at Memorial Stadium

When it became obvious this would be the last time Johnny would be able to play at Memorial stadium, the fans cheered for him to come on the field all day long. They wanted to see Johnny play one more game

1971 Super Bowl Champions at the Baltimore Colts' Johnny Unitas' Restaurant

here in Baltimore before he left. They all loved him so much. There were 55,390 people at the stadium that day. They were chanting, "We want Unitas! We want Unitas!"over and over again.

On December 3rd the Bills came to Baltimore and Marty Domres was the quarterback. He was Johnny U's replacement. On this memorable day of Johnny's last day of playing in Baltimore and Memorial stadium, Marty Domres ran a play himself instead of passing the football off to one of his teammates. When he did this he fell down and nicked his hip. Domres walked off the field like Walter Brennan.

The Colts were killing the Bills on this day. When the Bills quarterback threw an interception, it gave the Colts the chance to get the ball back. Sandusky went over to Domres and said, "The fans want Johnny in the game." Marty said, "I'm not going to tell him you tell him." Sandusky went over to John and said "Marty hurt his hip and he can't play, you have to go in." Marty pointed to his hip showing Unitas he was hurt. Johnny was upset and said to Marty, "You better not be faking it."

Johnny threw off his wrap and started to throw some practice balls. This meant he was getting ready to go in and play. Marty Domres said, "The stadium went wild. The fans would not stop clapping and sheering for Johnny. When Johnny went on the field it was the loudest roar ever heard at the stadium. It was one of the greatest moments ever at Memorial Stadium and for Baltimore Sports.

On the next play Johnny threw a pass to Eddie Hinton who ran it in for a 55 yard touchdown. It was the 4th quarter which helped the Colts beat the Buffalo Bills 35 to 7. It was enormous and the fans went wild and cheered for Johnny more. The sound was deafening. You couldn't hear yourself talk or think.

A small plane flew over Memorial Stadium carrying a banner reading "Unitas we stand." My cousin Tommy Tana was in the upper deck that day. He said it was a cold damp dreary day until old number 19 took the field. Several tears came running down many a fans face including my cousin Tommy Tana and me. The day was Sunday December 3rd 1972.

The NFL named Marty Domres the player of the week, but no one knew it. It was Johnny's last game with the Colts and all the attention was on Johnny. Marty was also named the NFL player four other times in his career.

After Joe Thomas sent Johnny U to San Diego, everyone was upset. They wanted Johnny to be sent to a more traditional team. They wanted him to be with a more mature team with a blue collar background. People wanted him to play with men who were determined to win the game. Instead Joe Thomas sent Johnny to a flashier team with younger players.

Johnny U provided more discipline to the young athletes. He wanted stricter rules and regulations by all sport players on all levels at the end of his storied career. He noticed a widespread drug use among his fellow players. This was reported in the Catholic Review; Johnny U. said "Drug use sets a bad example for kids."

The last game Johnny Unitas played for the Baltimore Colts as their quarterback was in Florida. It was against the Miami Dolphins on Saturday December 16, 1972.

On March 29, 1984 Bob Irsay moved the Baltimore Colts to Indianapolis. The CEO of the Mayflower Transit Company Mr. John Burnside Smith arranged for fifteen trucks to pack the team's property and colors. They hurriedly transported the team to Indianapolis. It was a cold dreary rainy snowy day when the Mayflower trucks left Baltimore for Indianapolis.

When Bob Irsay did this, he broke the hearts of many Baltimoreans. Fr. Joe Breighner wrote, "We have learned that it is greed not gratitude for past services that motivates many rich people." We felt betrayed because we gave our dollars and dreams to a team that was our team. Fr. Breighner also said, "Mr. Irsay is a tragic figure not a terrible figure. For his sake, I pray he gets whatever help he needs. For Baltimore's sake I'm sorry he did not get it sooner".

After many long years suffering one disappointment after another of being without a football team, finally Baltimore has a great football team. Baltimore waited and waited and agonized through one let down after another to have another football team. "The Baltimore Ravens"are now our Baltimore team. They have taken us to two Super Bowl Championships.

We now have Joe Flacco as our quarterback and he also comes into Sabatino's. He has taken us to a super bowls and beyond. He gets sacked so many times it's a wonder he hasn't gotten hurt more than he already has. We had the marvelous Ray Lewis who was the best defensive player a team could ever have. We have the best owner Mr. Steve Biscotti who also comes into Sabatino's. Jonathan Ogden is the only Raven inducted in the Hall of Fame. He still lives in Baltimore. He is also very active in the community. Terrell Suggs is a great line backer. Steve Smith was our great receiver. Jimmy Smith is our corner back.

Quotes from customers

As I waited on customers, I interviewed them on what they thought of what happened to Johnny U.

John Conrad said, "Irsay and Thomas did everything to dismantle the whole team. They traded off all the talent and broke up all the players. Mr. Conrad felt like someone punched him in his stomach when they traded Johnny U to San Diego. It was very painful. John Conrad said, "Back then you had to inherit tickets to go and see the Baltimore Colts play. You couldn't buy a ticket. This is what made going to see the Baltimore Colts play so exciting."

Johnny Unitas with my daughters, Michelle and Anna

Jerry Trout said, "When he went to the football games with his father it was an event. It was something they looked forward to every week. What they did to Johnny U was an embarrassment to the City of Baltimore. It dishonored Johnny U."

Alan Charles said, "If they could trade Unitas who was the greatest quarterback who ever lived, they could trade anybody." Alan said, "If Steve Biscotti owned the Baltimore Colts instead of Irsay, he never would have traded Johnny Unitas."

Sol Levinson said, "He should have stayed as a Baltimore Colt. They shouldn't have moved such a great player. It was a shame what they did to him."

Fred Frank said, "It was the beginning of the breakup of the Baltimore Colts. Johnny will always be remembered as a Baltimore Colt. He was quite a football player. He was famous in his own right."

Ed Attman said, "It was a bad move for Maryland and our team. It was unbelievable the way they let him leave Baltimore like that."

Mike David and Danny Lepfeld said, "It was heartbreaking they thought Johnny deserved more than what he got for all he did for Baltimore."

Bud Hammerman said, "It was the worst public relations move ever." Michael Olesker said, "It was horrible, his best days were behind him, but how could they let him get away."

Stu Weinstein said, "You don't trade an icon. He was like family, it was an awful move. He was a legend, the greatest quarterback that ever lived. For all he did for Baltimore they did a great injustice to him. He put Baltimore on the map and Irsay dismissed him like he was nothing."

Lou Getlan said, "It was disgusting, they should have kept him until he retired."

Barry Bronstein said, "I wouldn't accept the fact that he was gone. He should have finished his final years in Baltimore." The late Chip Silverman would have agreed with this also.

Lenny Wachs, "I thought they were jerks to do this to Johnny."

Bob Noel said, "They shouldn't have traded him he was Mr. Baltimore."

David Silverberg said, "They should have left him play his last years as a Baltimore Colt."

Arnold Posner said, "Johnny was the greatest quarterback that ever lived. He couldn't believe what they did to him they should have kept him forever." Mr. Posner used to lend cars to the Colts so they could drive around town. One time he was lucky enough to go to California with the Colts when they played the Los Angelos Rams. Arnold, Bruce, and Stuart Posner along with Wayne Berger partied the whole weekend with the Colts in California. It was the best time of their lives.

Johnny's children and my boss Renato's children all went to the same school together and they became friends. On one of the memorable evenings I worked at Sabatino's Johnny came into the restaurant. As soon as he came into the restaurant he asked my boss Vince where are my girls? When I came to work at Sabatino's, I brought my three other friends Marge, Rita and Jean. We all worked at Johnny U's restaurant. Johnny knew we all worked at Sabatino's. When he came into the restaurant he'd ask for us.

On one evening when the restaurant was extremely busy. Suddenly Johnny and his son Chad and Rick Volt came into the restaurant to have dinner. They had a very enjoyable evening. They received much attention from all of the customers who dined at the restaurant this evening.

When they were finished, Johnny placed his credit card on the side of the table. This meant he wanted his check. I avoided giving it to him because I knew if I did he would leave and I wouldn't see him for some time. The restaurant was so busy I really couldn't get to it at this time. When my boss Vince saw his credit card he said, "Peachy Johnny wants his check. "Well I was busy and I couldn't give it to him right then."

After a while my boss said, "Peachy I told you Johnny wants his check." I gave Johnny his check even though I hesitated to do this. I have always had premonitions in my life and I had a premonition if I gave him his check and he left I would not see him again. A couple months later Johnny passed away.

Johnny Unitas was a proud yet humble man. He never forgot his humble beginnings. This won him a permanent place in the hearts of all who ever knew. Because of his commitment to "give back"the Johnny Unitas Golden Arm Educational Foundation was established in 1995. It helps to promote football on all levels by providing financial aid to deserving young athletes. You can help to perpetuate Johnny's dream of helping young deserving athletes fulfill their dreams. If you wish to contribute feel free to do so. Bruce Laird was one of the many people who helped to make this establishment possible.

The neighborhood Johnny Unitas use to live in, Timonium, is now called "Legend Hill." One of the customers I serve was Johnny Unitas' upholster. His name is Jim Young and he lives in the same neighborhood Johnny Unitas lived in. This is how he got to do Johnny's upholstering. He is the person who told me they named the place Johnny use to live in "Legend Hill".

Jim told me when he went to Johnny's home he had two sets of coat hangers in the kitchen. One was in a usual spot for his older children and the other one in a lower position was for his younger children. Jim and Johnny remained friends for many years.

Another customer I served was a physical therapist student at Kernan's Hospital in 1969. Johnny U's therapist was William Neal and Howard Wagenheim was a physical therapist student there. When Johnny U came there for his physical therapy, Mr. Wagenheim met him.

After his therapy treatment Johnny would go outside and throw the football around. He played catch with the kids at the hospital. Johnny visited the children that were newly admitted to the hospital. The children who had casts on would get their casts autographed by him. Johnny was so good to children; he never turned any one of them down when they asked him for an autograph.

CHAPTER TEN

Haussner's

Another iconic restaurant in Baltimore was the famous Haussner's. Unfortunately it has been taken over by a construction company. They are making luxury apartments out of the area Haussner's was located in today. The address was 3236 Clinton Street.

My father wanted me to work at Haussner's because it was in my neighborhood. He said, "I could walk to work, and the restaurant was closed on Sunday and Monday." He said if you worked there you would be able to spend more time with the children and my Mom and him.

The famous German Restaurant, Haussner's, was located in East Baltimore for several years in Highlandtown. The restaurant seated about 500 people in the dining rooms on the first floor. The banquet rooms seated an additional 300 people and the restaurant was 30,000 square feet.

It was one of the top grossing independent restaurants in the United States which employed over 210 people. The art collection was world known and considered one of the best 19th century collections in the world. Mrs. Haussner loved to collect antiques.

Haussner's had the best food; everything was made fresh and home-made to order. They had German food, steaks, the best seafood dishes, and thirty-two different vegetables. They also had their fabulous home-made desserts, including their very famous strawberry pie and short cake.

The homemade muffins and rolls are the reason I gained so much weight while I worked at Haussner's. The lines wrapped around the block every evening. People waited in lines for long periods of time to eat their fabulous food.

On one memorable Saturday evening Haussner's served 25,000 people. This was a huge achievement. The employees made everything

Me holding a plate from Haussner's

homemade, the crab cakes, desserts, soups, regular potato salad and German potato salad right on the premises. There were two hundred items on the menu. It was the best restaurant in Baltimore.

They used 600 to 800 pounds of crabmeat every day. The crabmeat was used in their crab cakes and all the other seafood dishes they sold. No matter how much they made during the day, they always ran out on Saturday evening. They had to make more because Saturday was their busiest day. Mrs. Haussner's Mom owned a grocery store on Preston Street. This is how she got started in the restaurant business.

Originally, Haussner's was located across the street from where it operated for many years. It opened there in 1926. Mr. Haussner moved the business across the street where they were located for 72 years, over seven decades.

Haussner's was open seven days a week. During WW ll there was a shortage of man power so they closed on Sunday. Mr. Haussner also liked to go to church on Sunday. This was another reason the restaurant was closed on Sunday. All the recipes from the restaurant were from Mr. Haussner.

Economics determined a five day operation to be viable, so they closed on Monday starting in 1966. Interestingly the restaurant did more volume in five days then they had done in six.

One day Mr. Haussner saw a young man selling newspapers on the corner of his restaurant. His name was Jack, and Mr. Haussner asked him if he wanted a job working in the restaurant. Jack worked there for forty six years. Years later, when Mr. Haussner became sick, Jack's wife Mary who also worked at the restaurant as a hostess went over to Mr. Haussner's home. She read to him because he was blind. Mr. and Mrs. Haussner were wonderful people and they treated everyone kind. They were both smart and very intelligent people.

When Mr. Haussner was alive he would stand at the door as the waitresses left the kitchen to make sure the food looked presentable for the customers. If it wasn't, the waitress would have to take it back in the kitchen.

After Mr. Haussner passed, Mr. Bill took over the position as the manager. He stood by the door of the kitchen to inspect all the food that was going out to the customers just like Mr. Haussner did.

They had several hostesses seating the people in the different isles. The hostesses were just ordinary women who lived in the neighborhood. The hostess was very amicable towards the customers and the customers loved them. They seated the customers in all the different isles because there were many.

The line would go around the block every evening but it was especially long on Saturday evenings. The people started lining up at four thirty on Saturday evenings.

There was a little parking lot across the street from Haussner's. The lot could not accommodate the many people who came to Haussner's. The people who parked their cars in the neighborhood never got hurt while walking to Haussner's.

The neighborhood was very safe at this time because Highlandtown was a low crime area. It was a section of Baltimore that had all working class people who lived there. Most of the people owned their own homes. There was never any incident with any of the customers.

When the customers started to complain it was cold outside, Mrs. Haussner installed a heating system there. She wanted the customers to be warm. One evening the customers started to complain they smelt something burning. One of the women in line had a wig on and the heating system set her wig on fire. Mrs. Haussner paid for the women to buy a new wig. Eventually they let the customers come into the basement in cold weather.

In the basement there were more antiques and paintings. There was a big ball of string everyone came to observe. The ball of string originated from the string around the napkins delivered to Haussner's every day. When lunch was over all the waitresses had to fold boxes and boxes of napkins and cut dozens and dozens of lemons so there would be enough for the customers that evening. All the string around the napkins was saved, and the strings were added to the ball of string. It became so enormous the Haussner's put it on display. People could not believe it when they saw it.

The kitchen was a well-oiled machine There was a bar to order and pick up drinks. They had three bartenders at all times to serve the customers and the waitresses. The bar had pictures of woman revealing some of their private parts. Because of this, women were not allowed to enter it. Mrs. Haussner thought it was improper for women to see. The Haussner's only permitted men to enter the bar for several years. Finally after women protested they were allowed to enter it.

The kitchen was huge. When you passed the bar on the right straight ahead was the place where the cooks prepared all the seafood dishes. To your left is where the cooks prepared all the different meat dishes.

Ray Farrow Sr. and Jr. holding a plate from Haussner's

Past this were the 32 vegetables. Past the vegetables there was the fried food section, where the seafood and the eggplant, onion rings, and french fries were cooked. There was never a foul language used by anyone in the kitchen. Everyone respected everyone else.

Most of the employees worked at Haussner's for thirty years or more. They lived in the neighborhood and walked back and forth to work every day. Whenever an employee went up the Avenue the businesses on the Avenue treated them very good.

There were 40 people working in the daytime. They did all the preparations. They started working at seven o'clock in the morning. All the vegetables came from the farm. The employees cut the fish fresh every day. They had terrapin soup made from a real live turtle.

When one of the customers ordered the soup from my friend Marge Farrow, she asked the customer if she ever had it before. The women told her she would be fine. She asked Marge what makes you think I won't like it. When Marge brought it out to her she never touched it.

Some of the women who worked in the kitchen at Haussner's came in early because they had so much work to do. They came in at 7:30 and worked until 4:30. The night crew came in 4:30 and worked until 11:30 or 12 o'clock. Some of the kitchen people worked from 12 to 9. The cleaning crew came in at 4 AM in the morning until 11 o'clock. They cleaned all the statues and the pictures, the carpet, the kitchen, the bathrooms, and the museum upstairs. They worked from Tuesday to Saturday.

There was a watchman working there all night long even though the restaurant never got robbed. Only one time when the lights went out one woman tried to take one of the small statues, but she was never prosecuted. It was also the only restaurant that paid all their help in cash every Friday. Haussner's was the first restaurant in Baltimore to have a 50 year reunion. They took their employees downtown to the Inner Harbor to celebrate.

Ms. Dorothy Brown worked for Haussner's for sixty years. Because she was such a trusted employee she walked to the bank every night to deposit the money from the restaurant. She was accompanied by a police officer and Bobby Schunck and they never got robbed in all the years they did this.

When I worked at Haussner's I met my dear friend Marge Farrow. Marge and I were the only waitresses who were not married, and because of this we became close. She even got her two children Sherrie and Bobby to watch my children for me in the evening. I needed to give my Mom and Dad a break from watching them.

Sherrie and Bobby were young and they played with my children and my children loved them because of this. My children would put make up on Bobbie and curl his hair. He just let them do whatever they wanted to do to him. They got along so good with my children and they all had fun together.

The baker made 2,500 pumpkin pies for Thanksgiving and the customers lined up to buy the pies. David Burgess was the main baker at Haussner's for years. On Saturday evening when Haussner's closed M's Haussner would give the pies and cakes left over to the employees to take home.

She was a very generous person. She also took some of the cakes and pies and gave them to her neighbors. The young Tommy D'Alesandro lived in Guilford near her and she took his family pies.

There also was a worker named John Carter who checked all the orders in delivered to Haussner's. He cleaned the basement with bleach every night and made sure the place was clean.

Mrs. Haussner was a very stately woman and everyone treated her with respect. All the employees called Mrs. Haussner Mom she insisted on it. M's Haussner would get up some mornings at 4 o'clock and play the piano. She was the first woman who had a plane license. One time Mrs. Haussner asked me to take a ride with her. She wanted to go to Epstein's Department Store to buy something. When she drove down a one way street to get to Epstein, I reminded her what she was doing. She told me not to worry they know who I am. Mayor Schaeffer came to Haussner's to visit her many times.

She also had Chinese friends who owned Jimmy Wu's restaurant on York Road and they came in to visit with her all the time.

Mrs. Haussner donated a lot of property to the Salvation Army. She was the head of the community of the Church Home Hospital. She was the one who got all the bright lights put around the Hospital.

She went around the world five times and when she came home she would say, "There's no place like home."

Mrs. Haussner gave all the employees a paper weight for the 50 years Haussner's was open.

Haussner's is where I met another of my friends, Bobby, who started to work at Haussner's when he was 15. We have been friends for several years. He is one of my best friends and we talk almost every day on the phone. He did many chores while he worked at Haussner's. He was called the coffee boy. Bobby walked up and down the steps all night long and helped supply the kitchen in whatever it needed.

He carried all the ice upstairs four buckets during the night. He made coffee and cut the eggplant and helped the dishwasher when it was time for their breaks. He told me Haussner's used 50 packs of linen on Saturday Night. He carried them up stairs from the storage room up to the front of the restaurant. Bobby visited Ms. Haussner every Sunday when she was in Church Home Hospital.

He has memorabilia of many movie stars because he traveled to Las Vegas constantly connecting with many them. Two of his most famous connections were Liz Taylor and Debbie Reynolds.

When I went to Sabatino's I got Bobby a job there also. After I

Me & Bobby Schunck reminiscing about our days at Haussners

brought him to Sabatino's I worried they would not accept him. He had many hilarious ways about him, and he was also gay. Everyone who worked at Sabatino's, welcomed him with open arms. He always told stories and made everyone laugh. Bobby worked at the restaurant for many years. We are still good friends today. He calls me every day just to talk. He is my dear friend.

My friend Marge Modesto was a waitress who worked at Haussner's' also. She lives in the same neighbor as I do. She told me the reason she got a job at Haussner's' was because she could walk to work. This was the same reason my father told me to go and work there because you could walk to work.

Her sister lived in upper state New York. When Marge and her husband Eddie went to visit them and people found out where they were from they asked them about Haussner's. People from all parts of the world knew about Haussner's. It was known worldwide. It was known for fine food and fine art.

When Marge waited on a special couple, she commented on the ladies hands. The husband told Marge his wife was a hand model.

Another couple she waited on ordered crab cakes all the time. They also ordered crab cakes to go. They were missionaries and they took the crab cakes to the mission. Some of the hostesses who seated all the customers were Agnes, Tina, Maria, Mary, and Bernice.

Losing the Love of my life

During the time I worked at Haussner, my Dad passed away and I was traumatized. Who would have thought such a strong willed person like my father would die as young as he did at the age of 66? He was just beginning to enjoy his retirement. What a thrill he got when he received his retirement check. When he got his first check he said to my Mom, "Look Phyllis I got a pay check for doing nothing."

My Dad was a very prominent figure in my life and he always tried to steer me in the right direction. He always did everything for me. He told me there are only two things in life you have to do, you have to die and pay taxes. He recited proverbs to me all the time. He also told me if you don't have enough money to pay your bills, the one bill you cannot let go is your house payment. He told me if you don't pay your house payment they can put you out in the street.

It was hard for me to accept his leaving me at this time. His strength and knowledge helped me in my life and I needed him. I missed him so. He always told me to make sure I had good tires on my car, so I wouldn't have a flat tire while I was driving alone. He worried about me so.

One time he took my car for me because I needed a tire. When he did this they told him I needed a front end alignment and a wheel balance and four new tires. After he came home and told me, I was upset. I said, "Dad what am I going to do there was only enough money for one tire?" He said, "I know what you are going to do, pay a dollar down and a dollar when you catch me." This was from a man who paid cash for everything he bought. He used to call me the dollar down girl.

Now that I had lost him, what was I ever going to do without him? When Dad passed away my family and I went wandering and wondering what we would do without him. It was very difficult for all of us especially me, because he did everything for me and my children. I couldn't stand being without him.

My Mother was lost without him because they had been together for thirty nine years. He was the love of her life. When they looked into each other's eyes, they still had the lasting look of love, something you do not see today. He was such a huge presence in all of our lives we didn't know how we would be able to manage without him. He was everything to all of us. He was the most iconic person in my life.

Chapter Eleven

Sabatino's

Another iconic restaurant that was started in the 50's is Sabatino's. After working in many restaurants in Baltimore, my friends kept telling me you have to go to work in Little Italy at Sabatino's. My cousin Clara had a beauty shop in Highlandtown I went to. The barmaid from Sabatino's also went there. Her name was Mulkie. Clara's beauty shop was a neighborhood shop and most of the customers were repeat customers so therefore everyone knew everyone else.

Every time I saw Mulkie, she would say, "Why don't you come to work at Sabatino's. You'll do good there." It took me a long time to decide what to do. I didn't know how I could leave my children for such a long time. Who could I get to watch my children for all the hours Sabatino's was open? I had to consider this before I applied for a job at the restaurant. After I was certain to have capable baby sisters to watch my children, I went to apply for a job at Sabatino's.

Some of my baby sitters were my cousin Lucille and her sister Patty. They lived one block from me. They would spend the night and I would take them home in the morning.

The History of Sabatino's

The restaurant has recently celebrated their 50 years of being in business in the year 2005. Joseph Canzani and Sabatino Luperini became partners and joined their resources to open a small 50 seat Italian family restaurant in Little Italy. The restaurant now spans five decades and three generations.

When people found out about the delicious food served and the generous portions they were serving at Sabatino's, the restaurant became busy every evening. The restaurant grew and expanded in 1961, 1971, and 1981, eventually encircling three row houses and it now seats 450 guests. In 1968, Sabby retired and Joe added his nephews, Vince Culotta, Renato and Ricky Rotondo, all of whom had worked at the restaurant for years.

They learned the tradition Joe had taken so much pride in. Vince, Renato, and Ricky became partners in 1974, allowing Joe the opportunity to semi-retire. Sadly, Joe passed away in 1981, before the remolding of the new building was completed. Before Joe passed away he had picked all the design for the restaurant down to the light fixtures and table clothes and he had the tin ceiling restored.

Chef Joe trained Renato who continued the tradition of preparing the original family recipes with the freshest and finest available ingredients. Vince and Ricky became the familiar faces everyone saw extending a warm smile and a friendly greeting to all who passed through the front door.

In 1992, Ricky retired and left the business. Since then Vince and Renato, along with their children and other family members, have maintained the same quality service, and delicious Italian cuisine customers have known and loved for 50 years. Over these many years, generations of loyal customers and many dedicated employees have been the backbone of Sabatino's success. The children of Vince Culotta, Philip and Lisa, along with Renato Rotundo and his son Little Renato, work in the restaurant with their fathers today.

The restaurant has the best veal dishes (the veal Francese is tender pieces of veal cooked in a white wine, lemon, and butter sauce with just a hint of prosciutto ham). Their homemade pastas are tender egg noodles, or cheese ravioli, and gnocchi's which are the best little pieces of pasta made out of flour egg and ricotta cheese. They are so delicious. All the homemade pasta is made in the restaurant. The marinara sauce is simply superb.

Many other specialties include their fabulous clams' casino, and their fantastic garlic bread. The Shrimp Renato was created by Renato Sr. when Renato Jr. was born. It consists of shrimp cooked in a light brandy sauce with cheese melted on top and some prosciutto ham. You cannot get these appetizers anywhere else the way they are made at Sabatino's.

The Bookmaker Salad was created by a person who was a bookmaker during the day and a maitre d' in the evening at Sabatino's. He would go in the kitchen and make the salad for his friends. It consists of shrimp, salami, cheese, eggs, lettuce, tomatoes, onions, olives, and pepperoncini. When the regular customers saw the huge salad they wanted one. It is a meal in itself. It became so popular they put it on the menu. There are many more delicious dishes too many to mention. With all of these many superb dishes, the restaurant is busy every night.

The Many Celebrities coming to Sabatino's

With all the great dishes the restaurant has, it has enticed many movie stars, singers, and sports celebrities to come to the restaurant. When they performed in Baltimore, Sabatino's was the only restaurant opened late night to be able to have a dinner.

Al Pacino came to Sabatino's when he was filming the movie "And Justice For All." Barry Levinson was born and raised in Baltimore. He was the director of the film and the one who told them about Sabatino's.

The night before Al Pacino came to Sabatino's, he was down at Fells Point. The girls attacked him. They tore his clothes off. He had to get a police escort out of Fells Point. The next evening was Friday. Barry called my boss Ricky and explained what happened the night before. He told Ricky they were tired. He said, "We have just finished shooting and Al and Gene want is come in and have a quiet dinner."

Ricky came upstairs two times rubbing his chin which meant he needed a table. When he came upstairs the second time, I asked him what he needed. He took me aside and said, "Don't tell anyone Al Pacino is coming, he doesn't want to be bothered, so don't call your relatives."

My friend Kathy and I served Al Pacino, Jack Warden and the rest of the crew that evening. We were as calm as could be. Kathy was so young and pretty and all the actors were admiring her. She could have had her pick of any of them, but she was very bashful and shy.

I Am An American Day Parade

There was a parade every September held in Highlandtown called "American Day Parade." It actually started in Fells Point at Gough and Broadway. It then proceeded to Bank Street and down Patterson Park Avenue. It went all around Highland town's playground Patterson Park. My Uncle Mimi who was the City Councilman for our 46th district along with our fabulous Mayor William Donald Schaefer and many other elected officials were in the parade. One year Fonzie (Henry Winkler) and Ralph the Mouth (Donnie Most) from Happy Days were the Grand Marshals of the parade. When the parade was over, Buddy Palughi, the head of the Public Works Department, brought them to Sabatino's. I was lucky enough to be their server that day. This was another exciting evening at Sabatino's.

Frank Sinatra

Vice President Agnew frequented Sabatino's and became a close friend with my boss Joe. Joe was such a congenial man he got along with everyone. Agnew was elected Governor of Maryland but later he became the Vice President of the United States. The fabulous speech Agnew made at the Republicans Convention helped Nixon became President. After this Nixon picked Agnew as his Vice President.

After Agnew became Vice President he became friends with Frank Sinatra. The night Sinatra appeared in Baltimore Agnew brought Sinatra to Sabatino's for dinner. When Joe found out Sinatra was coming to Sabatino's, he had the whole upstairs dining room remodeled in one day. Sinatra had such a good time

Michael Armanti and guests at Sabatino's

at the restaurant because Joe fixed everything special for him to eat. Therefore every time Sinatra came to Baltimore he either dinned in or got food to carry out.

Cardinal Keeler with Judge Murphy and Judge Silver

When I was coming up the street to enter the restaurant, I noticed they were throwing debris out onto the fire escape. This was happening the night Frank Sinatra was coming to Sabatino's. After entering the restaurant I asked what was happening. At first no one would say anything, but after I was there for a while I found out Frank Sinatra was coming to Sabatino's. While I was waiting on customers, the workers were installing the new carpet. They were hammering the carpet down the stairs while the customers were dining.

When my friend Lill came in, the upstairs dinning was a mess, because of the remolding they did for Frank. She had to put it back together before Frank came. She had to do this in a hurry, but she managed to have it done in time before Frank came.

As Joe was cooking in the kitchen, he accidentally spilled tomato sauce on his shirt. He became upset because he had dressed immaculately for Frank. He wore a cream colored shirt, pants, and shoes to match. Once he got tomato sauce on his shirt, he tried to get the spot out of it but he couldn't. He had his shirt hanging up over the pots of boiling water in the kitchen to try to dry the shirt. When he couldn't do this he asked Mulkie the barmaid to call her husband Frank who lived across the street to lend him one of his shirts. After Mulkie called her husband Frank and told him Frank Sinatra was coming to Sabatino's, the whole neighborhood found out Frank Sinatra was coming to Sabatino's.

All the old ladies from the neighborhood were outside to greet Frank

Sinatra when he came into the restaurant. Don't you know he loved all the attention they gave him; it made him feel at home. He hugged and kissed all the old ladies from the neighborhood.

Joe fixed everything special for Frank to eat. He had a great time talking with his friends, the Agnews. Ralph Marceli, one of the people who helped remodel the upstairs dining room, was present at the dinner for Frank. He even sang a song to Frank about Veal Parmesan.

When Frank left the restaurant, he stopped in the room I was working in and yes his eyes were as blue as the sky. When he went outside, he was greeted by all his songs coming from the small sandwich shop across the street from Sabatino's. This was where all the bookies hung out. They had their doors open and pulled the juke box outside of the store. Frank's music spilled out into the streets of Little Italy. There was a huge crowd outside to greet him when he left. He was extremely happy to see all his fellow Italians cheering for him. Therefore every time he came back to Baltimore, he came to Sabatino's either to dine in or got carry out back to his hotel.

Vice President Agnew

When Agnew was accused of bribery charges while he was Vice President he had to resign from his post. He had to take care of his legal matters in Baltimore. As the trial was going on he pleaded nolo contendere. After he left the Federal Court house he came to Sabatino's to see his old friend Joe. He told Joe he came to Sabatino's because he wanted to be among friends. He knew he would always have a friend in Joe. When he was forced to resign, he came to see his friend Joe once again. He said, "Joe I might be looking for work."

Jerry Brown

One time Jerry Brown was running for president. After the polls closed, all the local politicians from Baltimore brought Mr. Brown into Sabatino's. On Tuesday evening after the dinner hour, we only work with a skeleton crew. Joe went home because it was Tuesday evening, his night off. The restaurant became so busy; my boss Vince called his uncle Joe to come back to work. He told Joe, Jerry Brown is in the restaurant please come back to Sabatino's.

When Joe came back to the restaurant he tried to come in the front door. The secret service men were guarding it and they wouldn't let Joe enter. Joe was standing at the front door saying Vince, Vince they won't let me in my restaurant. Finally Vince came to Joe's rescue. He told the secret service men to please let Joe in because he had to cook for Jerry Brown. This was another fantastic evening at Sabatino's.

Joe's Leisure Time

My boss Joe worked very long and hard hours at Sabatino's. He only took off on Tuesday evening. Joe would go down the block because there always was a card game there. While he was there he made friends with many of the owners from the clubs on the infamous block. One of Joe's friends was Sammy Goldstein who owned one of the clubs on the block. Through Sammy, Joe met many of the other club owners.

As soon as the club owners closed their business they always came to Sabatino's. It was the only place in town they could get a good meal. Sabatino's would be packed at 2 o'clock from all the club owners and strippers from the block. When they came to Sabatino's, they didn't order anything small, they ordered steaks, lobster, and pork chops, all big dinners.

When Sammy left Sabatino's around four o'clock in the morning, the last people, who spoke to him, were Ralph Marceli and Pete Galliano two local residents of Little Italy. When Sammy arrived at his home gangsters were waiting for him. They shot and brutally murdered him.

Here are some famous people who came to Sabatino's:

Ted Kennedy

Because Mayor Tommy D'Alesandro lived in Little Italy many politicians came to Little Italy. When Ted Kennedy was running for President he came to Sabatino's for lunch. After my boss Vince met Mr. Kennedy he was shocked to know Mr. Kennedy knew Johnny Pica. When Vince asked him if he knew Mr. Pica, this is what he said, "I don't know him, but my brother Jack told me when you come to Baltimore, you have to look him up. He will show you a good time in Baltimore."

Vince called Johnny Pica and asked him to come to Sabatino's. When Johnny came in, Vince introduced him to Ted Kennedy. During this time Ted Kennedy was running for President. Jimmy Carter was also running for President. During his campaign Jimmy Carter also came into Sabatino's to dine and I was privileged enough to serve both of them.

President Jimmy Carter

After Jimmy Carter became President, he came back to Baltimore to visit Little Italy. One of his associates was friends with Mr. Chiapparelli. When President Carter came back to Baltimore his associates took the President to Chiapparelli's. The streets of Little Italy were packed during this memorable day.

A cameraman from DC was outside of Sabatino's. My boss Vince was also outside looking at all the excitement. The cameraman asked Vince if he could come into the restaurant to get something to eat. The cameraman told Vince the secret service wouldn't let him in Chiapparelli's. Vince told him, "That's okay. Come in here and eat something." After he finished his lunch, Vince told him he didn't have a check.

When the cameraman left the restaurant, he asked Vince if he ever read the *Washington Post*. Vince told him he didn't read it. The reporter told Vince I think you should get it tomorrow there will be something in there you will like. When the *Washington Post* came out the next day, there was a picture of President Carter walking in the streets of Little Italy. Behind the President was the huge sign of Sabatino's. The quote in the paper said, "President Carter dined in Little Italy."

After Mr. Chiapparelli saw the paper, he called my boss Vince and said, "You bum, President Carter ate at my restaurant and the paper made it look like he ate at yours."

Governor Marvin Mendel

Governor Marvin Mendel frequented the restaurant often. Ted Levitt of Chick & Ruth's Deli brought the Governor in often. On one occasion when the Governor came in with Ted, I interviewed him. I asked the Governor how he was able to take the initiative to stop the chaos that was happening during the gas shortage. Even though he was older, he still had the ability to answer all the questions I asked him. He was very knowledgeable of the politics of the current day. Governor Mendel came to Sabatino's many times during his many years of being Governor.

Johnny Depp

On one of my late night evenings, while working at the restaurant, a huge limousine pulled up outside of it. Many young people came into Sabatino's. It was around twelve o'clock in the evening. Patty was another waitress and she and I served them. We set them up and started to take their orders. As I looked into this one person's eyes, I almost dropped my note pad. It was the one and only Johnny Depp. I have always loved him because he had the prettiest eyes similar to my husband. I couldn't believe he was here, I was so excited.

Johnny Depp was in town making the movie "Cry Babies." After they finished shooting, they came into the restaurant to get something to eat. They were all young people and they were all dressed a little shabby. The Maitre d' just thought they were a bunch of kids out partying. This was another wonderful evening while working at Sabatino's.

Will Smith

Many famous people came to the restaurant while they were appearing in Baltimore. Will Smith came in before he married Jada Pinkett. Jada's family lives in Maryland and that's why Will Smith was in Baltimore. The evening he came into Sabatino's was a Friday evening, around 8 o'clock. Will and his friends came into the restaurant on the evening he was going out on the town with his friends before he married Jada.

When they were seated all the employees knew immediately who he was. It was all over the restaurant in no time at all. He had such a good time at the restaurant he smiled from ear to ear the whole time he was at the restaurant.

Keanu Reeves

When Keanu Reeves came to Baltimore to make the film, "The Replacements"at Camden Yards, he came in the restaurant to have dinner. I stood next to him when he came to the bar to get a drink. He is a very handsome man and extremely tall. Although I didn't have the opportunity to serve him, he was very friendly while he was at the restaurant.

Debbie Reynolds

All the guys who were performing with Debbie Reynolds at the Meyerhof came in the restaurant on a Friday evening. It was my good fortune to be able to serve them. When I found out who they were working with, I asked them if they would please bring her into the restaurant before they left. On Sunday evening after their last performance they brought Debbie Reynolds to Sabatino's. Renato fixed her food special. We took pictures with her and talked to her for some time. She had a great time while she was here. She laughed and kidded with the guys who performed with her. She talked to everyone and my bosses Vince and Renato took pictures with her. She was just as nice and pretty as she looked when we saw her in pictures as she looked in person.

Kathleen Turner

Kathleen Turner also came to Sabatino's after her performance in Baltimore. She is very beautiful. When she came into the restaurant Vince and Renato talked to her for a long time. Renato fixed her food special for her. We took pictures of her with my two bosses. She stayed at the restaurant for some time. She liked the food so much she came back the next evening with her husband and child.

Shaquille O'Neil

Shaquille O'Neil also came to the restaurant. He was in a swimming match competing against Michael Phelps for charity. When he came to Sabatino's, he ordered five dinners. Renato could not believe he was going to eat all the food. He went upstairs to talk to him and to his surprise he did eat all the food. He had a great time while he was at the restaurant. The waitress serving him was Lynn. She told him Michael Phelps was going to beat him in the swimming match.

Ed Harris and Woody Harrelson

Ed Harris and Woody Harrelson also came to the restaurant. They were making a movie about Sarah Palin in Baltimore. They liked the food so much they came back many evenings the whole time they were filming the show.

Debbie Reynolds and cast from her show at the Meyerhof at Sabatino's

Kathleen Turner and Vince Culotta, owner of Sabatino's

Stevie Wonder

Stevie Wonder came to the restaurant when he performed at Pier 6. He performed in the place of Aretha Franklin because she was sick. I served him and told him I loved his song,"You are the Sunshine of my Life." I told him when my children were little, I sang his song to them all the time while we were riding in the car. He ate Chicken Lynn in a white sauce. The whole time he was in the restaurant he swayed back and forth like he did while he was singing. He had a wonderful time while he was at the restaurant.

Mohammad Ali

Mohammad Ali came to the restaurant while he was in town and he was extremely friendly. He went into the kitchen to talk to all the cooks and shook their hands. The cooks were so excited to see such a great person.

The Wrestlers: Rick Flare

All the wrestlers from WCW and WWF come into Sabatino's when they came to town for their met. When the wrestlers come into the restaurant they filled the entire restaurant. Rick Flare came into the restaurant whenever he was in town. When he arrived at Sabatino's, he brought all his entourage after their meet at the Baltimore Arena. Rick Flare was crazy but it was in a good way. He always had a great time at the restaurant. All the crazy things he did while at the restaurant people still talk about today.

When the other wrestlers came to town, they always filled the whole restaurant. There were so many of them I never realized there were that many wrestlers. All of the groupies and fans followed them into the restaurant also.

Macho Man

He also came to the restaurant often. One evening six wrestlers came into the restaurant. Five of them were tall and huge with big muscles. One of the men was shorter but had muscles also. When they were there for a while two drunken men came into the restaurant. The two drunken men tried to pick a fight with the wrestlers. I tried to calm the wrestlers down because the section they were sitting in has mirrors all around the dining room.

When I couldn't calm the wrestlers down, I went to get the manager to stop the fight. All the time I kept saying to the wrestlers please calm down. I told them please don't pay attention to them. The smallest wrestler said in his very distinctive voice, "Don't tell me to calm down young lady." After he said this, I finally realized who he was. The smaller wrestler was Macho Man; because he was out of his costume I didn't recognize him.

Eventually the cops came and locked up the two guys who started the fight with the wrestlers. After the cops locked up the two guys, the wrestlers calmed down and finished their dinner. This was the end of another exciting evening while I was working at Sabatino's.

The Rock

One Friday evening The Rock and many other wrestlers came into the restaurant after their met at the Arena. They were seated on the Mezzanine because they were a large group. Ms. Marion and I waited on all the wrestlers. We had no idea who they were. All we knew was how very polite and mannerly they were the whole time we were waiting on them. The Rock was one of the wrestlers. He treated Marion and me great. The Rock and all the other wrestlers were very mannerly and respectful. He left us a huge tip. This was another memorable evening at Sabatino's.

Andre the Giant

Andre the Giant was seven feet five inches tall and weighed 400 lbs. He came into Sabatino's after a match at the Civic Center. He ate a large amount of food and drank a gallon of wine. He was seated in the bar room and he took up the whole table. After he ate, Renato, one of the owners and also the chef, came out to talk to Andre. He asked him if he like the food. While they were talking Renato said to Andre, "You really put on a good act while you wrestle."

After Renato said this to Andre he became infuriated. Andre wanted to take Renato outside and punch his lights out. Some of the regular customers had to calm Andre down. Clem Florio, the sports writer from the race track and Rick Flare another wrestler were in the restaurant at this time. They helped to calm Andre down. Later Rick Flare told Renato not to worry about Andre because he was a little crazy.

The Local Celebrates

A customer from Sabatino's Gary Huddles, said his cousin, Phil, lived with him. Phil's mother was Gary's mother's sister and she passed away. This was the reason Phil lived with Gary and his family. Gary was only seven years old and Phil was like his big brother. Phil would go out with his friends in the evening. When he came home it would be around four o'clock in the morning. Phil woke Gary up. Gary asked Phil where you go so late in the evening. Phil told Gary he went to Sabatino's. Phil told Gary Sabatino's is the place to go after every place in town is closed. Phil told Gary everybody goes there after the clubs close. When Gary turned seventeen, he came to the restaurant, and when he came there he could feel the presence of his cousin Phil.

This was one of the reasons the restaurant became so popular. After people had been out for the evening and were hungry, the restaurant was the only place you could go to get good food. They told all their friends about how great the food was. This is how come the restaurant became so busy. It was all word of mouth with no advertisement.

Here are some of the wonderful people I served who have helped me through the many years; I have worked at the restaurant.

Josh Charles was a star of the Good Wife. He has also starred in many movies. He comes to Sabatino's after he goes to see the Orioles or the Ravens play. He is originally from Baltimore. His father Alan has an advertising company. His uncle Stan Charles has his own sports show. His uncle Ron Matz is a local TV news reporter. They all

Barry and Jane Bronstein at Sabatino's

come into the restaurant when Josh is in town and have dinner together.

Because I always waited on Alan Charles and his family, he asked me to be in one of his commercials. Alan made a commercial with the managers and coaches of the Orioles. Mike Hargrove was the manager during this time. There was also Elrod Hendricks, Terry Crowley, and Rick Dempsey. The thing that was so funny about the commercial was they all ordered their food the same way they gave signals to the players. After they ordered their food in sign language, I repeated what they ordered in English. It turned out to be a funny commercial. It was a lot of fun doing it.

After making the commercial for Alan, I met Father Bob Albright. He frequented Sabatino's with his students from Towson.

While waiting on Father Bob he asked me if I was the person in the Oriole commercial. I told him yes I was. This started a wonderful relationship between Fr. Bob and me.

I also have been waiting on Dr. Michael Sanow who is a professor at Catonsville Community College and his family for quite some

Josh and Alan Charles and Jim Palmer at Sabatino's

time. While waiting on Dr. Sanow I found out he was friends with Father Bob.

Fr. Bob teaches inter faith religion. He and Dr. Sanow have been friends for some time. Through Dr. Sanow he introduced me to the most wonderful man Mr. Leo Bretholz.

Mr. Bretholz was a holocaust survivor. He told me many stories of how he survived. They were too unbelievable. Mr. Bretholz escaped from Hitler four times.

Through the relationship with Dr. Sanow & Fr. Bob we established a lasting friendship with Mr. Bretholz. It was marvelous being in the presence of these three learned men.

These friendships started because of the commercial I made for Alan Charles.

Barry Levinson the famous director and producer from Baltimore also frequented the restaurant. He made many films in Baltimore and in other cities. He was always congenial when he came to the restaurant. He never forgot his friends at Sabatino's. Whenever he was in town, he frequented the restaurant.

One evening I approached him for some advice about my books. He told me I had to add a lot of drama. He said Hollywood loves drama. With his advice, I added drama to my books.

When Elaine and Steve Kennedy come in the restaurant, they are accompanied with people from the Little Italy association. Angie and John Curria are the couple who come in with the Kennedys. They are such comical people, always joking and kidding around. They are so much fun to wait on because they always make me laugh. No matter what they are talking about the conversation somehow turns to the topic of sex.

The other people who always make me laugh when they come into are Carole and Stanley Alpert. No matter what the topic of conversation is about it always turns to sex.

Mr. Wachs was friends with Mr. Amanti's manager. He told the manager when Mr. Amanti comes to town we will come and see him. After the performance, Mr. Wachs told the manager and Mr. Amanti's he knew a great Italian restaurant to bring them to. They all came into Sabatino's for dinner. He was a very gentle and congenial person.

After they ate, Mr. Wachs told Mr. Amanti this room loves your singing. They would die to hear you sing. He then got up and asked the people if it would be okay if he sang to them. They all said yes, so Mr. Amanti sang "O Solo Mio"to all the customers in Sabatino's. The performance he did was simply amazing. All the customers applauded for him after his performance.

Years later when Mr. Wachs saw his friend the manager of Mr. Amanti, he asked him whatever became of Mr. Amanti. The manager told him he became a country and western singer.

Aloma's Ruler

Another exciting evening at Sabatino's was the evening when Reds Scherr's horse Aloma's Ruler won the Preakness stakes at Pimlico in 1982. A horse trainer John J. "Butch" Lenzini persuaded Mr. Scherr to buy the two year old at an auction for $92,000. The horse was the son of Iron Ruler and Native Charger mare Aloma. Aloma's Ruler suffered an ankle injury in February 1982. Mr. Lenzini suggested not running the horse in the Preakness. Mr. Scherr overruled the trainer and ran the horse anyway. Reds had the pleasure of seeing his horse, ridden by jockey Jack Kaenel. He won the race at odds of 6 to1.

The most exciting thing about the horse was it was not the favorite to win the Preakness. Linkage was the favorite. When Mr. Scherr's horse Aloma's Ruler won, it was an upset. When Reds was interviewed by a reporter from *The Sun* in 1996 this is what he told him. "If I had to pick one race in the whole world to win, the Preakness was the race I wanted to win." He didn't care about the Kentucky Derby, or the English Derby.

He also told the reporter, "It was the most exciting moment in sports, maybe the most exciting moment in my life."

Mr. Nathan "Red" Scherr got his nickname from his full head of red hair. Red's whole family and his wife Annette's whole family came to Sabatino's after the Preakness. The whole first floor dining room in the restaurant was filled with all of their relatives. Mr. Red brought the blanket of the Black Eyed Susan into the restaurant and hung it up in the dining room. Because of this exciting horse race, the Scherr family brought a memorable evening into Sabatino's.

Aloma's Ruler also won the Withers Stakes, the Jersey Derby, and the Bahamas Stakes.

Norris Ford

One of the regular customers who came to Sabatino's was the Cook family. They owned and operated Norris Ford in Dundalk. It is a hundred year old business which opened in 1917, by his great grandfather George R. Norris. Mr. Norris was friends with Mr. Henry Ford. Mr. Ford thought the area the car lot began was a great location because Bethlehem Steel was not far from his dealership. The area their car lot is located in is the home of many car dealers. After they were there for some time, they enlarged their business to include the Honda line of cars.

The original owner was Landy Cook; they named their dealership after their son Norris. Norris now owns the car business along with his two sons David and Brian.

The people who came to work at Norris Ford never left. The people who work at the dealership helped to build Norris Ford up to where it is today. The owners treat their employees wonderful. To show their appreciation to all their car salesmen, they had Christmas parties at Sabatino's for them every year.

Mr. John Arend was the general manager of the car salesman. He arranged the parties to show their appreciation to the car salesmen. The menu for the car salesmen was the top of the line. It turned out to be such an elaborate affair they continued these Christmas parties every year.

One Sunday afternoon Norris brought many of his golf friends into Sabatino's after the PGA golf tournament. They all had the green jackets on after the golf tournament. Three to four men dressed in Scottish tilts playing bag pipes also came into the restaurant. They marched upstairs and into every room in the restaurant playing the bag pipes. They played the bag pipes until they went out the front door. Norris and his friends Jack & Digger and several of his other friends stayed for dinner.

The Card Reader

One evening a young customer came into the restaurant. While I was serving her we began to talk. I asked her what she did. She told me she read cards on the side. She asked me if I would like to have my cards read. I told her yes I would. I asked her if she could come back on Sunday evening around ten o'clock because it is slow then.

Earlier that evening Joe's brother, the Baron, or Tony as he was called, asked Joe if he could borrow twenty dollars. There was a card game across the street Baron wanted to get in. Joe lent Tony the money for the card game.

Later that evening the card reader came in the restaurant to read my cards. When my boss Ricky found out what she did he said, "Oh no, he said, you have to read my cards first." Then when Joe found out what she did, he told her she had to read his cards first. Finally she was able to read my cards. At the end of each of our card reading she told all of us a man in uniform was coming to see us. We had no idea what she meant because none of us knew a man in the service.

Later that evening when Ricky went outside, he saw the police climbing the wall of the sub shop across the street from Sabatino's with sawed-off shot guns. Many older men came out of the building and were being put in the patty wagon to go downtown. Ricky was handing the older men that were being locked up, shots of VO. They were handing Ricky their money. They didn't want to take the money downtown. The police treated the older men as if they were hardened criminals. When all along all they were doing was playing cards together.

The Lovers

Gabriella worked for Di Pasquale and was my sales representative when I had my shop. After she left Di Pasquale's she worked for another food distributor. She came to Sabatino's to sell them food products. After my boss Renato found out she was Italian and single he arranged for her to meet, my other boss Vince's son Phil. After they met and dated for some time, they fell in love and got married. Gabriella and Phil had a huge sign made to thank Renato for bringing them together and hung it in the kitchen. The sign said "Thank You Cupid." They now have three lovely children, two girls Adriana and Maria, and a little boy whose name is Vince, after Phil's father Vince.

I waited on so many people who became engaged while I worked at the restaurant. The restaurant has become the restaurant where lovers come, ever since the Disney movie "The Lady and the Tramp." When they ate the spaghetti and meatballs and their lips almost touched. Many young couples come into the restaurant. Because of this movie, they think Sabatino's is a romantic place to come. In fact there is one table in particular on the mezzanine and after the dinner hour is over, it is quiet and secluded. It is near the window and very romantic up there. Hardly anyone is seated up there late night. This is the table where many young couples become engaged.

The late night crowd

Many evenings, while working at the restaurant till three o'clock in the morning, people would fall asleep in their food. It became so funny their heads would land right in their plate of spaghetti and meatballs. Then we would have to get the manager to come and wake them up. Other times some of the customers would try to start fights with other customers. Many nights I would get in the middle of the people to try to break the fight up. I became friends with many of the late night customers because they became regular customers.

Two of the people I became friends with were Dan and John Bondroff two brothers who would come into the restaurant after the bars closed. They came in with many of their friends. One evening while I was waiting on Dan, John, and their friends, two other guys came in and started to pick a fight with the two brothers, for no reason at all. Naturally the two brothers got up immediately and were ready to fight these two bully guys along with the other guys at the table. I didn't want anything to happen to the boys I had been waiting on for months. I stood between my two customers and my two young men. I told the two bully guys to leave. I told them to get out of the restaurant and wouldn't let them hit on the two brothers my friends. They listened to me and left the restaurant so therefore that was the end of what could have been a big situation.

Since this incident their mother Joyce and Barry and the father's brother Stanley and his wife Rita have become regular customers of Sabatino's.

Chapter Twelve

Patterson Park

All of my family, friends and neighbors were fortunate enough to have our own playground right in our back yard. It is the lovely Patterson Park. We used the park for many different events like baseball, tennis, soccer, and swimming. It was fabulous. There were also concerts in the park during the summer months that many people enjoyed. Now I will tell you a little history about our beautiful Patterson Park.

In January 24, 1827 Mr. Patterson wrote a letter to the then Mayor of Baltimore, Jacob Small. He offered to donate the land to the City of Baltimore. It was 5.96 acres of land called "A Public Walk." The land where Patterson Park is today was in foreclosure. Mr. Patterson bought the land cheap from Nicholas Rodger. Mr. Patterson then gave the land as a gift to the city for the purposes of having public recreation for the people of Baltimore.

Mr. Patterson arranged for the planting of some two hundred trees in a straight row. It was the first park in the City. It is the oldest park in Baltimore. In 1852 the public walk was named Patterson Park in honor of Mr. Patterson.

Before it was named Patterson Park, the land was known as Harris Creek. Boats would sail from the Harbor (were the Korean War Memorial is located today) up Harris Creek right into Patterson Park. The water came right into the City all the way up to Harris Creek which was located in Patterson Park. The Historical stream Harris Creek was put under ground in a huge brick tunnel. After they did this it was hidden from view. No one even knew it was there until today.

The Harris Creek watershed actually covers a geographical area from Clifton Park all the way down to the Inner Harbor. It came down past Johns Hopkins Hospital to Patterson Park. It then went down to the Harbor in Canton.

My Uncle Mimi Di Pietro at the American Day Parade

Harris Creek was a site of a number of essential boatyards. The "USS Constellation" and many clipper ships were built here. They supplied not only jobs but sailing vessels which kept Baltimore a vital and essential port of call. All the vessels were used in the War of 1812. Harris Creek played a key role in Maryland's history and the U.S.

Patterson Park became the most aggressive Park in the nation. Patterson Park is a 175 year old neighborhood common with English picturesque add ones. There is a Victorian add on and also a playing field. They never did the park over they just kept altering its character. Patterson Park remains most significant because it is Baltimore's most intensely used large park. It remains and outstanding example of the 19th century park design. The site is surrounded by extensive row houses. The neighborhood relies solely on this park for open space.

Baltimore purchased an additional thirty acres of land and continued to improve the park until 1861 which was the start of the Civil War. During the Civil War the park was used as a hospital cite for soldiers who fought during the war. The solders camped out in Patterson Park. The Park also served as the USA General Hospital. It was called Camp Washburn.

After the Civil War, there were no improvements made in the park. In 1853 Patterson Park was designated a formal city park. The first allotment of money for the park was then handed down. A picket fence was proposed and erected around the public walk.

When the "War of 1812"began, it interrupted the plans to fix the park. The war forced a hold on any further developments until its conclusion.

Improvements began after the camp was razed from the Civil war. This created a larger community park for the surrounding neighborhoods. Land was acquired and new facilities were built in the style of the Country Park. Downing, Olmsted and Daniels were the people who suggested this be done. Baltimore architect George Aloysius Frederick, was the designer of City Hall. The City's Board of Park Commissioners hired him to develop the park's first structures. He created the Marble fountain, the gate house, and the Lombard Street entrance pillars.

In 1860 Patterson Park experienced its first expansion when some 29.21 acres were purchased from Patterson's heirs. Monies were appropriated to fence and grade the new parcel of land.

In 2002 through the City and State, the Friends of Patterson Park and some private donors they were responsible for the reconstruction of the historical Pagoda. The rededication celebration had one hundred saxophonists playing there that drew thousands of current and former neighbors. The four story oriental style tower is made of fabricated iron supports, wood and glass. The ornamental building has three observation decks with a spiral staircase leading to each. The perception from the top deck is one of the best in Baltimore with views of Canton, the Inner Harbor and downtown.

Some People who improved Patterson Park:

The Olmsted Family

Frederick Law Olmsted had a major intellectual influence on the development of parks to serve the needs of nineteenth century American cities. The firm of Frederick Law Olmsted and his sons Frederick Jr, and

The Bicentennial March

John Charles were the leading park architects of the day. According to the Olmsted report, the twenty acre extension was acquired, consisting of relatively level landscape to the east of the older sections pastoral slopes.

Between 1905 and 1918 the Olmsted Brothers' firm developed plans for the new section of the park, where their principal designs were for active recreation facilities, a field house, swimming beach, and bath house, playground, and ball field. In Patterson Park you can see the two sides of the Olmsted vision, the sweeping hills by the senior Olmsted as well as the active recreation movement.

The park is coming alive today more people than ever are doing things in the park. Families are planting trees and there are concerts near the Pagoda. Both aspects of the park are being used. The Olmsted's' ideas between urban green space and recreational facilities are both being used in Patterson Park today.

Charles Latrobe was born in a house on Calvert Street in 1833. He apprenticed under his father Ben Latrobe II as an engineer for the B&O railroad. His cousin Ferdinand Latrobe was elected Mayor of Baltimore in 1875. Charles was appointed Chief Engineer of the Jones Falls Commission. He designed the combing walls that directed the Jones Falls through the City. Charles also engineered arches. Charles created the Pagoda in 1891, and the Casino buildings in Patterson Park.

There is a monument below the Pagoda. The Star Spangled Banner Centennial Memorial rests a few paces northeast, were several more cannons flank the area. The location provides an impressive view of the park and City and beyond.

Ferdinand Latrobe was elected to seven terms as Mayor in 1895. Ferdinand acquired the estate of Johns Hopkins that eventually became Clifton Park. His statue is on North Broadway near East Baltimore Street.

Betsy Patterson

When Jerome Bonaparte came to Baltimore, Joshua Barney invited him to come to the races at Havre de Grace on the Susquehanna. Joshua told Jerome he was going to introduce him to the prettiest girl he would ever see. Betsy Patterson was the daughter of William Patterson the wealthy shipping merchant. Jerome was anxious to met Betsy because of the way Joshua described her to him. While everyone was watching the races, Jerome had his spy glasses on Elizabeth.

After they met, Betsy wanted to see Jerome again. Jerome also wanted to see Elizabeth more and more. After Mr. Patterson found out about Jerome and Elizabeth and their chance meeting he made Betsy go to Springfield at her mother's summer home. When Betsy found out Jerome was going to be at the Chase Ball, she rode a mule all the way to Annapolis which is twenty miles. She wanted to be at the ball Jerome was going to attend. Jerome had dinner at Brooklandwood with the Richard Cantons. Mr. Carroll, whose name was Carrollton, was one of the persons who signed the Declaration of Independence. Mr. Carroll was Baltimore's first citizen. He escorted Betsy onto the dance floor. Mr. Carroll presented Lieutenant Bonaparte to the loveliest girl in America. Jerome bowed to Betsy and asked her for the next dance. Even though Betsy had promised the dance to someone else, she danced with Jerome. Later he took her out into the garden where they spent hours together. He told Betsy he wanted to kiss her. After this evening he told her she would not dance with another man ever again.

When her father found out about what happened, she received much backlash from him. Betsy would not give up hope and finally her father gave in to her. They were married on Christmas Eve in 1803 by the Mayor of Baltimore John Carroll, the first Catholic Bishop in the United States. She was only seventeen when she married Jerome Bonaparte who himself was only eighteen years old.

Unfortunately when Napoleon Bonaparte found out about this he was not happy. He condemned their marriage and ordered his brother Jerome back to France. He demanded the marriage be annulled. In 1804 Jerome and a pregnant Betsy traveled to France in time for Jerome's brother's coronation.

When they arrived in France Napoleon denied Betsy permission to set foot in Europe. Jerome sent Betsy to London and told her he would reason with his brother. Jerome traveled to Italy to attempt to reason with his brother. He wrote Betsy saying he would do everything he could do to bring them together once more. She never saw Jerome again. Their son was born on July 7, 1805 in London.

Jerome gave into his brother and returned to France and married the German princess Catharine of Wurttemberg on August 22, 1807 in France. (His marriage to his dearest Elsa had not yet been dissolved.) Betsy returned to Baltimore with her son who she called "Bo." In 1815 by special act of the Legislation in Maryland she secured a divorce.

CHAPTER THIRTEEN

Johns Hopkins

My friend Sherrie gave me a huge book about Johns Hopkins when I told her I was going to write about the Hospital. The book is enormous. It has details of the beginning of the hospital and college. While researching, I found many details that started this wonderful establishment. I hope you will enjoy the information I discovered. They have helped many people from yesterday until today.

Johns Hopkins was born on May 19, 1795 to his parents Samuel and Hannah Hopkins. They were Quakers and owned a 500 acre tobacco plantation. He was born in Whitehall, Maryland on his family's tobacco plantation in Anne Arundel County.

The homestead known as Whitehall stands near what is known today as Crofton, Maryland. The family's plantation was granted by the King of England to their ancestor Will Hopkins in the 17th century. His parents had slaves work it for them. In 1807 the leaders of the Society of Friends preached slavery did not agree with their faith. Samuel Hopkins then freed all his slaves.

The Hopkins named their 10th child Johns Hopkins after his great grandmother's maiden name Margaret Johns. Most of his brothers and sisters had Janney in their names.

Johns at the age of 12 had to leave school and work the fields. Although his education stopped his learning, his mother encouraged him to continue his studies. He continued this at night in the dark. He had a sharp mind for figures. His mother told him he had business ability and he should go where the money is.

His father's brother Gerard owned a grocery store. Hopkins was an apprentice of his Uncle's grocery store at the age of 17. After he worked there he increased his Uncle's business considerably. He lived with his uncle Gerard and Aunt Dolly for seven years. While there he fell in love with their daughter Elizabeth. She was only16 at the time. They couldn't marry because they were cousins. They vowed never to marry anyone else. They remained friends and later Johns Hopkins bought her a home near his own. He bequeathed it to her upon his death. She died in 1889.

In 1819 Hopkins began his own wholesale business. In 1822 he forms Hopkins Brothers wholesale firm. He used three of his brothers as salesmen. The firm grew rapidly. It did business in Maryland, Virginia, and North Carolina. One of the early fortunes of Johns Hopkins was moonshine whiskey. Hopkins agreed to take moonshine in return for good. He re-bottled it and sold it as "Hopkins Best." The first year he was in business he sold $200,000 worth of goods. In 1835 he retired at age 40 as the head of his multi-state wholesale merchant enterprise.

Hopkins lived in downtown Baltimore on 81 W. Saratoga Street. In 1835 Hopkins purchased a mansion that is now known as the City's Clifton Park Golf course at 2107 St. Lo Drive. His home was known as Clifton. He hosted visitors like the Prince of Wales who was later King Edward VII. Clifton was sold to the City in 1895. Hopkins mansion served as the golf course Club House.

In 1845 he become a prominent Baltimore banker, and finance capitalist. After he invested in the B & O railroad, he became the director of it in 1847. He was a powerful member on the board of the B & O railroad the nation's first railway. In 1857 there was a financial panic in America. Hopkins pledges his personal fortune to ensure the solvency of the B & O railroad. He saved Baltimore from financial ruin.

In 1861 during the Civil War Hopkins overcame the Southern sympathizer board members. He put the B & O at the service of the Union. Then he met with Abraham Lincoln to discuss the war. Hopkins sent the President a note offering advice about keeping the peace. During the Civil war the population of Baltimore was split between the North and the South. Southern sympathizers attached the Massachusetts Regiment on Pratt Street near the Inner Harbor on April 19, 1861. While they switched trains in Baltimore on their way to DC., four soldiers and twelve civilians were killed and dozens were wounded. Baltimore remained under the control of federal forces for the rest of the war.

In 1866 Hopkins friend George Peabody opens an institute for a music academy, library, and art gallery.

Johns Hopkins asked the General Assembly of the Maryland legislature, in 1867 to establish two corporations, The Johns Hopkins Hospital and The Johns Hopkins University. He virtually pledged his entire fortune to them which was worth seven million dollars then. It is worth $11 billion today.

The personal generosity of John Garrett's daughter Mary ensured the opening of the Johns Hopkins School of Medicine. In 1867 Johns Hopkins incorporates both his University and his hospital together. This was his wish.

The Hopkins Hospital was the first Hospital in the nation equipped with central heating. The corners were curved to avoid the building of dust and dirt. It had a ventilation system to guard patients from contaminated air.

In 1873 Hopkins states the hospital must provide for the indigent of the sick. It should have no regard to sex, age, or color. During another national stock market panic, Hopkins once again pledges his fortune to back the B & O railroad to prevent financial ruin.

In 1875 Daniel Gilman was chosen the first president of the Johns Hopkins University. This begins the official opening of the University. The ceremony was held at the Peabody Institute where the Peabody Orchestra performed. Gilman made sure Johns Hopkins will become the first research oriented graduate University in the United States. It was based on German and other European institutions of higher learning.

In 1876 John Billings was chosen to spearhead the construction and design for Johns Hopkins Hospital. He also created the School of Medicine. He worked with Gilman to select the original faculty. In 1878 the ground was broken for the Johns Hopkins Hospital. Because of the financial weakness of the B & O Railroad, Hopkins depended on for funding; the construction took thirteen years to begin.

Florence Nightingale was called the Lady with the Lamp. This was because of her service on the battlefield during the war with Britain. Her judgment was valued by Mr. John Billings. She sent sketches for the nursing school for Hopkins Hospital. Billings showed her notes to the Hopkins trustees.

The Death of Johns Hopkins

In the headlines of *The Baltimore Sun* on Christmas Day they wrote about the death of Johns Hopkins. On December 24, 1873 Johns Hopkins dies at his resident at 81 West Saratoga Street in Baltimore. He lived to be 88 years old and never married.

The opening of the Johns Hopkins Hospital was in 1889. After a dozen years of periodically construction interruptions, on a sunny mild day it opened. It was considered a national marvel. It was the largest medical center in the country. It had seventeen buildings, there hundred thirty beds, twenty physicians and two hundred employees. Its motto was "For the good of all who suffer."

The four doctors, who were the founders of the Johns Hopkins School of Medicine, were William Henry Welch in charge of pathology. William Stewart Halstead was in charge of surgery. William Osler was in charge of internship. Howard Kelly was in charge of gynecology. They continue to fascinate historians and inspire physicians for decades even after their deaths.

In 1886 pathologist William Welch opens a pathology lavatory and launches the first graduate training program for physicians in the County. He was also the first Dean of Hopkins School of Medicine. He was responsible for getting it up and running in less than a year. He was a valued mentor and he acquired the nick name of "popsy"by his residents and fellow doctors. He became president to nineteen major scientific organizations. He had the power to transform men's lives almost by the flick of a wrist.

Welch invites surgeon William Stewart Halsted to come into his pathology laboratory. They were friends from the New York Bellevue Hospital. He was a graduate of Yale and the Columbia University College of Physicians and Surgeons. Halsted spent three years developing the methods known as "Halstead School of Surgery." He developed a sterling reputation as a surgeon, diagnostician and advocate of techniques aimed at avoiding infections. He is appointed the first surgeon in chief of Hopkins Hospital in 1890. He was the first professor of surgery in the School of Medicine in 1892. He battled addiction to cocaine, with which he had experimented on himself in 1884. He was testing its potential as a local anesthetic. Although his self-experiments advanced the course of early anesthesia, this affected his health for the rest of his life.

In 1888 Internist William Osler was premier clinical physician and a superb teacher. He was the first professor of medicine and physician and chief of Hopkins Hospital. Osler later creates America's first medical residency program to the training of American physicians.

Billings did not waste much time on pleasantries when extended a job offer. Billings showed up one day at his Philadelphia apartment. Without sitting down, he asked me abruptly, "Will you take charge of the Medical Department of the Johns Hopkins Hospital?" Without a moment's hesitation he answered, "Yes." Billings left and told Osler to see Welch about the details. "We are supposed to open soon. I am very busy today, good morning." At that Billings was off not having been in the room for more than a couple of minutes. He famously observed, "He who studies medicine without books sails an uncharted sea, but he who studies medicine without patients does not go to sea at all".

Gynecologist and surgeon Howard Kelly one of the first founding physicians was among the first physicians to use radiation as a cancer treatment. Kelly was a fervent fundamentalist. Christian Kelly is credited with establishing gynecology as a true specialty. He concentrated mainly on developing new surgical approaches to women's diseases and to understanding the underlying pathology of them. He invented numerous medical devices, including a urinary cystoscope and what is known as the "Kelly clamp", a scissor-like forceps with a locking mechanism and no teeth. It was used for holding tissues during gynecological surgeries. When radium was discovered, Kelly was among the first to try it for cancer treatment. (Some sources say he got a sample directly from Marie Curie). He founded his own Kelly Clinic in Baltimore. It was once the nation's leading center for radiation therapy.

Henry Martin was a distinguished scientist. He was a brilliant Irish born biologist and physiologist. He was one of the first researchers ever to receive a degree in physiology. He was a protégé of Thomas Huxley the British biologist known as Darwin's Bulldog. Martin established the first American biological laboratory and developed a well-organized premedical and graduate training course. It was called the called Chemical-Biological Program. Martin's program was shown by the excellence of his students.

John J. Abel became the School of Medicine's first professor of pharmacology. William Henry Howell became the first head of the Department of Physiology. Martin was expected to fill this position. His deteriorating health due to alcoholism made him resign from Hopkins in 1893. This was right before the medical school opened. He returned to England and died three years later, at the age of 47.

John Jacob Abel was America's first full time pharmacologist. Among his achievements was inventing the first artificial kidney. He called the machine's process vivid diffusion. It allowed the removal of blood cleansing it and returning to the animal. Although it was successful it wasn't used on humans until decades later. Abel ignored accidents and ailments. In 1900 a laboratory explosion caused glass to destroy his right eye.

Hopkins first chief radiologist Frederick Baetjer was devoted to exploring radiology. He over-exposed himself to radiation before its dangers were understood. He lost all of his fingers and one eye. He planned to continue his work as long as he lived fingers or no fingers.

William Howell had a Ph.D. in physiology. He was the only one who did not study abroad. He was an accomplished researcher an influential mentor. He became dean of both the School of Medicine and then the school of Hygiene and Public Health.

He wanted to become a physician but lack of funds prevented this. He left Baltimore to become head of the physiology department of the University of Michigan. Then he joined the faculty of Harvard.

He was called by Gilman to return to Hopkins brand new medical school. He headed the School of Medicine and the School of Public Health. He was among the first researchers to suggest that the two lobes of the pituitary gland are functionally different. He provided evidence of a chemical nature of the nervous influences that control the heart rate.

Franklin Mall was the first professor of anatomy. He turned his lecturing duties over to subordinates. He wanted to test his student's memory not their intelligence. He wanted his students to become independent scientists. Each of his students was assigned to a part of the body. He expected them to figure out the principles of anatomy independently. He is known for his work on the heart, liver and spleen. He also established a research institute for embryology.

Hopkins was the first major medical school in the United States to admit women on an equal basis with men. This was due to the insistence of a group of women. Mary Garrett was the daughter of founding Hopkins trustee John Garrett. Mary Garrett herself contributed the bulk of funds $455,000. Ms. Garrett's generosity, allowed women the education in a man's profession, after the long denial for them. She stipulates the school be a four-year graduate school for men and women. They need to be admitted without distinction between them.

In March of 1892, Dr. Henry Hurd recommends a separate ward for African American patients be built. Many other hospitals did not accept. The building accommodated 56 patients. Special care was taken to see the heating and ventilation was perfect. A sun Balcony was erected on each floor for convalescents. The building was fire proof throughout.

Sir William Osler was the founding physician in chief of Johns Hopkins Hospital. He was the first director of the Department of Medicine. He was born in Canada and knighted by Great Britain's King George V.

He had a close connection to an American Found Father. In 1892 Osler married Boston-born widow Grace Revere Gross. She was the great-granddaughter of Paul Revere. He was the Boston silversmith best remembered for his famous April 1775 ride to warn patriots of the approach of British troops. Paul Revere warned the American people the British were coming one-hundred seventeen years ago.

In 1898 William Osler obtained Hopkins first grant for medical research when an anonymous donor gives $750 a year for five years for the study of tuberculosis.

Hugh Hampton Young was a 27 year old resident in surgery at Hopkins. His boss told him he was chosen to specialize in urologic surgery. This was a field he knew nothing about. He learned quickly. His invention of pioneering methods and surgical implements for treating enlarged inflamed prostates and removing cancerous ones. This earned him international renown. A New York surgeon quipped "The prostate makes most men old, but it made Hugh Young."

Harvey Cushing came to Hopkins in 1896. He brought a hand cranked X-ray machine. He introduced the use of X-rays in preparation for surgery. He also monitored blood pressure during surgery. He helped Hopkins gain international reputation. He discovered the hormonal function of the pituitary gland. He founded the medical specialty of endocrinology. He became the director of the nation's first experimental surgery laboratory. Cushing wrote the first definition text on neurosurgery and developed it as a specialty.

Pathologist Simon Flexner was a protégé of William Welch and William Osler. He advanced through academic ranks to a professorship in pathological anatomy. There was a dispute over the then unspoken but general refusal to promote Jewish faculty. He left Hopkins in 1899 to become professor of experimental pathology at the University of Pennsylvania for two years. He was named the first director of the Rockefeller Institute for Medical Research.

Pioneering hematologist Maxwell Wintrobe established the modern methods for measuring a blood sample volume of red and white blood cells and platelets. The Wintrobe hematocrit was the most commonly used instrument for performing these measurements. He single handedly wrote Clinical Hematology, the most authoritative work in the field. Yet in his thirteen years at Hopkins due to its subtle but pervasive anti-Semitism, he never advanced beyond the rank of associate physician. He left to become head of the department of medicine at the University of Utah. He immediately jumped from the lowest academic rank to the top.

Walter Dandy spent his entire professional career at Hopkins. He was a surgical genies and an emotional person in the operating room. He developed new methods on brain tumors, cranial nerve, lesions, and injuries. Meniere was a disease (an inner ear disorder causing dizziness). It caused vascular lesions in the brain as well as surgery for spinal cord tumors and ruptured inter-vertebral discs. The magnitude of his contributions to neurosurgery is recognized every day at Hopkins and around the world.

In 1900 three protégés of William Welch, Walter Reed, James

Carroll, and Jesse Lazear were members of the U.S. Army yellow fever commission in Cuba. They discovered mosquitoes transmit the disease. Reed was head of the commission. Lazear died of yellow fever which he contracted during his experiments. The commission's work is considered one of the greatest achievements of modern medical science and it virtually eradicates yellow fever.

Curt Rechter spent 60 years introducing the term "biological clock"in a 1927 paper describing his observations of the cyclical internal mechanisms that drive the eating drinking and sexual behavior of animals.

In 1904 on February 7th the great Baltimore Fire destroyed seventy investments properties most of them warehouses. The building had provided annual endowment income to the hospital. In May the hospital receives a letter from John D. Rockefeller Jr. It stated in view of the high character of work which the hospital and medical school are doing in medical research including training of nurses, my father will give five hundred thousand dollars to Johns Hopkins Hospital. It is the first of many donations the Rockefellers gave to Hopkins.

In 1912 multi-millionaire James Brady nick named "Diamond Jim"- came to Hopkins to see surgeon Hugh Hampton Young. Surgeons from Boston and New York refused to operate on him. He was worried. He had complicated factors. He had diabetes, high blood pressure, angina, and kidney failure. Brady thought Young was his last chance for treatment to ease his prostate problem.

Dr. Young told Brady he just invented an instrument (the Young punch) to operate on him. Young injected cocaine into his urethra as a local anesthetic. Young did not make any external cut. Jim Brady did not have to have anesthesia. Dr. Young handled with skill the Young punch and removed the troublesome prostate. Brady was off the table in no time at all. Then he considered Young his best buddy.

Young proposed to Brady he should consider funding a urology institute. Young told Brady it would carry his name forever. He sold Brady on the idea. On January 21, 1915, the eighth floor was named the James Buchanan Brady Urological Institute. When Brady died he bequeathed another $300,000 to maintain his name.

The Wilmer Eye Clinic

The vivacious daughter of wealthy Cuban parents Aida de Acasta was the person determined to open the Wilmer Eye Clinic. She lost the sight in one eye and Wilmer treated her. She decided in 1922 to create the Wilmer Clinic. She contacted many former patients who had been treated by the charismatic Wilmer. By January of 1925 all but $100,000 of the necessary $1.5 million was raised. The Johns Hopkins hospital decided to make up the difference.

In 1946, a movie version of M's. Susie Slayer was made. It was about the lives of Johns Hopkins medical students who lived in a Biddle Street boarding house.

Miss Susie counseled a number of aspiring young Hopkins doctors. The movie inspired many would be physicians to apply to Hopkins. Even though Hopkins wouldn't allow his name to be used in the film, people knew it was about Hopkins.

After graduating from high school my Mom and Aunt Mary Del Guidice went to work at Johns Hopkins hospital. The year was 1931. My Mom was 18 years old. Mom and Aunt Mary were allowed to stay in the house on Biddle Street because they had to be there very early in the morning.

They became servers to the nurses and doctors who lived at the hospital. These people were the interns at the hospital. Mom told me they had to wear white gloves while they served the nurses and doctors. Mom had to stand and watch them to see if they needed anything. If they did my Mom or Aunt Mary would get it for them.

For years, my Mom always told me she didn't want to go out to eat. She told me she didn't want people watching her while she was eating. I never understood this until I became a waitress. The waitresses have to watch their customers to see if they need anything. All these years I thought Mom didn't want other customers watching her eat. When all along she didn't want the waitresses watching her eat, because she was once a server. Finally I understood what she meant.

Dr. Levi Watkins Jr. as a child was baptized by the Reverend Ralph Abernathy, a civil rights leader. As a teenager, Watkins participated in the

1955-1956 Montgomery bus boycotts, a pivotal moment in the US civil rights movement. The 381-day citywide boycott of public transit was led by Dr. King. This was sparked after the arrest of Rosa Parks. She refused to give up her seat to a white passenger. Later she volunteered with Dr. King.

Watkins earned his bachelor's degree from Tennessee State University. After graduating with honors from Tennessee State in 1966, Watkins became the first African American to be admitted to and graduate from Vanderbilt University's School of Medicine. He later completed a surgical internship at Johns Hopkins Hospital.

Later he went to Harvard Medical School of Physiology. There he investigated the relationship between congestive heart failure and the rennin angiotensis system. He came back to Hopkins in 1970 as an intern in surgery.

In 1980 he ultimately became the first black chief resident in cardiac surgery. He was a pioneering surgeon renowned for performing the world's first implantation of an automatic heart defibrillator. He placed it in a 57 year old woman patient.

In 1991 Watkins was promoted to full professor of cardiac surgery and dean for Postdoctoral education in America by helping to establish the nation's first postdoctoral association. In 1992 the Vanderbilt University established a Professorship and Associate Deanship in Dr. Watkins' name to honor his work for diversity in medical education.

He joined with another African American colleague ophthalmologist Earl Kidwell to begin a successful nationwide drive to recruit talented minority students to Hopkins. He was determined to ensure they too had opportunities in the field. Dr. Levi Watkins changed the world with his passion for medicine. He not only impacted the field of medicine but he also inspired African-Americans to become doctors. He broke down the color barrier at two of the nation's leading medical institutions.

In 1982 Watkins founded the annual Martin Luther King Jr. commemoration at Johns Hopkins Hospital. Many times Dr. Watkins brought an extraordinary array of speakers to the campus for the event. Among them have been Coretta Scott King, Rosa Parks, Rev. Jesse Jackson, Rep. Kweisi Mfumi, Maya Angelou, Harry Belafonte, James Earl Jones,

Danny Glover, Lou Gossett Jr., Cicely Tyson, and Stevie Wonder.

Watkins dined at Sabatino's often. One night after an event at the Meyerhof Hall for the Heart Association Dr. Watkins brought Harry Belafonte with him into Sabatino's. It was a very exciting evening. Harry Belafonte had such a wonderful time that evening. The next time he came back to Baltimore he came into Sabatino's once again.

Watkins was an associate dean for postdoctoral affairs. He has been the driving force behind the ongoing diversity initiatives. At the celebration honoring his three and a half decades at Hopkins in 2006, he said, "I came up when color was everything." After looking at the diverse crowd that came to honor him, he said, "Looking out at all of you today, I don't see color at all." The people who were there honoring him were black, white, Asian, male, female, young, old, gay and straight.

Hopkins Hospital, and Health System President and Hopkins Medicine Executive Vice President Ron Peterson praised Watkins as a medical pioneer. He has been a role model extraordinaire and all around humanitarian. Ironically enough Dr. Levi Watkins passed away with complications from a stroke which led him to have a heart attack. What an awful loss for Baltimore. He was a wonderful surgeon with a fantastic personality. He was simply an amazing person.

Otolaryngology

A self-described "music addict"otolaryngologist Charles Limb has the rare distinction of holding faculty appointments at both the School of Medicine and Hopkins' Peabody Conservatory of Music. In collaboration with fellow researchers at the National Institute of Deafness and other Communication Disorders, he had conducted innovative studies that use functional magnetic resonance imaging. (MRI) tracks how jazz performers' brains react when they're improvising. Music, Limb notes, represents the pinnacle of hearing-an art form as complex in structure as language. It can provide important insights on how the human brain processes auditory information.

As a cochlear implant specialist, Limb foresees his studies of "the brain on jazz"could help him improve how deaf individuals with cochlear implants perceive music. He also believes a musical ear exam – rather than the current use of simple sounds such as blips and pings – might be sensitive enough to detect hearing loss at early stages or detect defects in pitch or tone standard tests may miss.

Limb's expertise in both hearing and music led to his collaboration with Baltimore Symphony Orchestra music director Marin Alsop and others in a special February 2008 program, "Beethoven: CSI." The orchestra performed excerpts from all nine of Beethoven's symphonies. The Limb and the other participants discussed that might have caused the composer's hearing loss and how it may have affected his music.

Dr. Ben Carson was the Pediatric neurosurgeon professor of oncology, pediatrics, plastic surgery and neurological surgery. The New York Times wrote about him becoming a folk hero. He has the impact which goes far beyond the operating room.

Ben Carson and his wife Candy went to Australia because the opportunities for him were better there. He had a chance to become a senior resident. Because of his association with the Church of the Seventh day Adventist, they both were welcomed to Australia with open arms. The people from the church gave them many things they needed for their upcoming baby.

An extremely difficult case came to his attention. This case changed the direction of his work. The woman had an acoustic neuroma. It is a tumor growing at the back of the skull. It caused offenses and weakness of the facial muscles. It would eventually result in paralyses.

He asked the senior consultant if he would mind if he tried using a microscopic technique. He did not get any approval from the senior consultant. The surgery took ten straight hours. The tumor was removed and the cranial nerves were saved. The woman thought the senior consultant had performed the surgery. After this surgery all the other physicians asked him to cover surgeries for them.

Dr. Carson said that in his one year there he got so much surgical experiences. My skills were tremendously better. It made me more capable and comfortable working on the brain.

"When I returned to America the chief of surgery at Provident Hospital wanted me to come there. I declined his offer because I knew Johns

Hopkins was where I wanted to be. On returning to Hopkins, I started getting many referrals. The chief of pediatric neurosurgery left and went to Brown University. Dr. Long proposed me to the board and I became the new Chief of Pediatric neurosurgery."

Miranda

"After this appointment a case came before me of a little girl named Miranda. She had lesions on the left side of her brain. She needed a hemi-spherectomy. If she didn't receive it, she would surely die.

I did a lot of consulting with Dr. Freeman. I read a lot of literature and went over Miranda's CT scan. I told Dr. Freeman I thought it might be possible. The operation took ten hours. Little Miranda's brain was very inflamed. Wherever my instruments worked, she started to bleed. Slowly carefully for eight tedious hours, I inched away the inflamed left hemisphere of Miranda's brain. Miranda lost nine pints of blood. I thanked God for wisdom and for helping to guide my hands.

As we wheeled Miranda down the corridor her parents heard it. Terry Franciscas said "wait." Miranda's eyes fluttered and opened for a second. She said, "I love you Mommy and Daddy." The nurse said she talked. I never thought she would be awake that soon. She was talking, hearing, thinking, and responding. We had removed the left half of her brain. This is the dominant part that controls this special area. Then she stretched her right leg and moved her right arm. This was the side I removed that controlled them. It was amazing the operation was such a wonderful success. It was unbelievable."

Separating the Twins

When Theresa Bindar got the news she was giving birth to Siamese twins, she wanted to kill herself and the twins. Later she made peace with herself. The babies' physicians in West Germany contacted Johns Hopkins. They asked if the pediatric surgical team could devise a plan to separate the Binder twins. After studying the available information Ben Carson agreed to do the surgery. Dr. Mark Rogers coordinated the massive undertaking. They spent five months of intensive study and training preparation for the surgery.

Dr. Carson's crew of doctors flew to West Germany to insert an inflatable silicon balloon under the scalps of the babies. This device gradually would stretch the skin. This would allow enough tissue to close the huge surgical wounds. They spent five months in planning through every contingency. A ten page play by play book detailed each step of the operation.

After anesthetizing the twins, heart surgeons Reitz and Cameron inserted a hair thin catheter in major veins and arteries. They cut into the two skulls carefully preserving the bony tissue holding the two skulls together. They preserved the bony tissue holding the skulls together. It would be used later to reconstruct their skulls.

When they started the cut below the area where their sinuses meet they experienced a large amount of bleeding. They sewed muscle patches into the area. They realized the torqula covered the entirety of the backs of both of their heads. It was gigantic.

Slowly they removed blood from the boy's bodies. This deep degree of hypothermia brings metabolic functions to a near halt. This allowed stopping the heart and blood flow for one hour without causing brain damage. After this the twins remained in a state similar to suspended animation. Then they had to work quickly. The procedure could only be done if the infants are under eighteen months. The brain is still developing then. It is flexible enough to recover from such a shock.

"After the skulls were open, I prepared to sever the thin blue main vein in the back of the twin's heads carrying blood out of the brain. Then we pulled the tables apart and Dr. Long had one boy and I had the other. For the first time in their little lives Patrick and Benjamin were living apart from each other. After this all we had was one hour to complete our work and to restore the blood flow."

The two doctors completed the work in time. There was intense bleeding. Their brains began to swell. This helped seal off the bleeding. By the time the operation was over the twins used sixty units of blood. This was a historic operation, "If the infants continued to recover," Dr. Dufresne planned a second operation to create cosmetic surgery. Dr.

Carson told the reporters the twins had a fifty-fifty chance. Dr. Carson repeatedly said, "It is all in God's hands." In 1989 both of the twins celebrated their second birthdays.

Transplants

Hopkins has become known as "Kidney Swap Central." Surgeon Dorry Segev and his wife, mathematician Sommer Gentry, solve problems to match multiple kidney transplants. This has been known as domino surgeries. Hopkins performed the first double and triple domino transplant surgeries.

Transplant chief Robert Montgomery oversees the multihospital transcontinental three-way swap transplant. There were ten, twelve, and sixteen patient surgeries often involving other hospitals and making Hopkins the United States "Kidney Swap Central." It currently is estimated that of the 60,000 U.S. patients now on a waiting list for a matching kidney, some 3,000 could die before getting it. Montgomery has developed a "daisy chain" strategy for kidney swaps. If fully implemented with a functioning national Kidney Paired Donation system, it could increase the annual number of successful transplants by 2,000.

Hopkins reputation for groundbreaking research and its important role in the Baltimore community were memorably combined by the crack of a bat and the cheers of a nationwide audience. On September 6, 1995, Baltimore Orioles shortstop Cal Ripken Jr. surpassed Yankee legend Lou Gehrig's 2,130 consecutive games streak. He then presented Hopkins researchers with a $2 million check to continue their quest to conquer amyotrophic lateral sclerosis (ALS). This was the neurodegenerative disease that killed Lou Gehrig and the disease has ever since been linked to his name.

The Orioles owner Peter Angelo spear headed the creation of the Johns Hopkins ALS Lou Gehrig Fund. The initial $2 million gift was raised by selling special, on-the-field seats to Ripken's record-breaking game at the Orioles' Camden Yards stadium. After Ripken retired from baseball since 2001, special sky box seats for his final game were also sold to help support Hopkins' ALS research. Ripken continues contributing to the fight against the invariably fatal disease.

The research is conducted now by the Robert Packard Center for ALS. It is headed by neuroscientist Jeffrey Rothstein at Johns Hopkins. It was named after Mr. Packard from San Francisco for his $4 million fund to combat ALS. Rothstein was treating Mr. Packard at the Packard Center. It is the only institution in the world dedicated solely to curing ALS.

Cal Ripken and his wife Kelly also have been generous supporters of the Johns Hopkins Children's Center. In 1997 Kelly herself founded the Kelly G. Ripken Program in Hopkins division of endocrinology to provide background information and education for patients with Graves' disease. It is a thyroid condition for which she has been treated successfully at Hopkins since 1993.

Some of the Women of Hopkins

In 1998 Ron Peterson and his vice president for operations appointed Karen Haller, a Ph. D. She was the director of nursing for the Department of Medicine for the past five years. Haller had master's degrees in nursing and patient care services. She won grants from the National Institute for Nursing Research. She had a triple threat credentials in research, teaching, and patient care which is the Hopkins prizes.

Christine White had been executive assistant for two deans D.A. Henderson in the school of Public Health, and Michael Johns in the School of Medicine. He added executive assistant to her title in 2007. She loved organizing managing and figuring out a way to accomplish what people think can't happen.

Ron Peterson also appointed Judy Reitz as executive vice president and COO of the Johns Hopkins Hospital. She became the first woman to hold that post.

In 1999 Ronald R. Peterson, president of The Johns Hopkins Hospital and Health System, appointed Judy Reitz. She was already a senior vice president of operations for Hopkins Hospital. She was chief architect of its ongoing operations restructuring as executive vice president and COO of the Johns Hopkins Hospital.

Reitz sought to bridge what had been a longstanding gap in understanding between the central hospital administration and the decentralized (and fiercely independent) functional units. They are made up of clinical faculty and headed by the medical school clinical department directors and their administrators. Reitz recognized that what often can be seen as Hopkins' maddening decentralization also is among its greatest strengths. She saw no reason however why Hopkins couldn't be run as an efficient organization while retaining its unique, invaluable attributes. She continues to strive to see that it does both.

Carol Greider is the director of the Department of Molecular Biology and Genetics, received the Nobel for her 1984 discovery of telomeres, and enzyme that preserves telomeres. Telomeres often likened to the protective plastic tips on chromosomes. Telomerase prevents telomeres from degrading when cells divide. The finding established the groundwork for subsequent studies showing that the enzyme plays a major role in cancer growth and conditions related to aging. The scientists' ultimate goal is to see if they can develop therapies that could affect the action of telomerase.

For Greider, the Nobel Prize that she shared with her mentor, biologist and physiologist Elizabeth Blackburn of the University of California, San Francisco, and geneticist Jack Szostak of Harvard, served as vital confirmation of the importance of basic, curiosity-driven science. All three also had shared the 2006 Lasker Award for Basic Medical Research frequently called the "American Nobel" for Greider's discovery and the groundbreaking research that Blackburn and Szostak did on telomeres.

For Greider, the Nobel Prize that she shared with her mentor, biologist and physiologist Elizabeth Blackburn of the University of California, San Francisco, and geneticist Jack Szostak of Harvard, served as vital confirmation of the importance of basic, curiosity driven science. All three also had shared the 2006 Lasker Award for Basic Medical Research frequently called the "American Nobel" for Greider's discovery and the groundbreaking research that Blackburn and Szostak did on telomeres.

The Nobel and Lasker are, Greider says, "a testament to investing in people who have clever ideas that might not seem directly applicable to diseases but become apparent later on." Not a significant part in the growth of cancer cells. Its link to degenerative diseases related to aging was uncovered long after that.

Greider was the daughter of scientist parents. Her father was a physicist. Her mother was a biologist. Her mother died when Greider was six. She had dyslexia as a child, struggled in school and was placed in remedial classes. "She thought she was stupid."

She had difficulty reading and spelling. She honed her already exceptional ability to memorize. This skill helped her excel in chemistry and anatomy, which she enjoyed. At the University of California in Santa Barbara, she earned a bachelor's degree in biology in 1983. She then obtained a Ph. D. in molecular biology in 1987 from the University of California at Berkeley. It was there that she became a protégé of Blackburn. She had enthusiasm for research into telomeres was contagious.

While working in Blackburn's lab she began searching for the elusive enzyme by studying a cell called Terrahymena. She worked on this for nine months. On Christmas Day 1984, she was working alone in the lab she pulled an X-ray film from the developer and saw something. There in the images was the exact pattern researchers had predicted would be seen if the unknown enzyme was found. After this Grinder and Blackburn conducted countless tests to make sure they hadn't made a mistake. Sparking and explosion in telomere and telomerase, they published their results and the rest is history.

"The Spirit of the Place"

The founding of the Johns Hopkins Hospital in 1889 and the Johns Hopkins School of Medicine in 1893 has maintained the same spirit after all these years. Hopkins has sought, nurtured, and been a magnet for men and women. They were drawn to the standards of Sir William Osler, from nearly a century ago. It is called "the spirit of the place."

In April of 1912 the Hopkins environment, which Ron Peterson spoke of remains what Hopkins big four would recognize immediately.

At the Hospital's twenty fifth anniversary in 1914, Osler wrote,

"Hopkins unique atmosphere, bound together everyone connected to the Hospital and medical school. It created a comradeship, sympathy with one another, and devotion for them to work were its fruits are."

Welsh said, "All who are here today from those early years, feel there was an environment and atmosphere of ideas. They will always be cherished and continue to influence future residents." Johns Hopkins Medicine continues to lead the way in every aspect of patient care, medical education and scientific research.

While working at Sabatino's, I had the privilege of waiting on many people from Hopkins. I asked two recent graduates from the University what was the best thing about Johns Hopkins University. This is what they told me. Arguably it is the best medical system out there. It has the best research by far in medicine with medical devices and biomedical engineering.

Later while waiting on two nurses from Hopkins Mary and Marlyn, I asked them what was the best thing about Hopkins. They told me Hopkins has worked with some of the best medical minds in history.

Redonda Mill is the first woman president of Johns Hopkins

Chapter Fourteen

The Baltimore Sun Paper

The Baltimore Sun, whose pages have chronicled Maryland life and its institution for generations, whose reporters covered every government and conflict and glory of the city since long before the Civil War, celebrated its 175th anniversary in 2012.

Ever since Vol. 1, No. 1 rolled off 30-year-old Arunah Shepherdson Abell's press on Wednesday, May 17, 1837, the newspaper has never been without its Sun vignette, or name plate, bearing the words "Light for All."

The concept of "Light For All" embodied Abell's philosophy that his newspaper would cover the news for all, not just for Baltimore's moneyed, banking, legal or merchant classes, but the common masses.

Abell, who had been born and raised in East Providence, R.I., worked as a shipping clerk before becoming an apprentice printer at the Providence Patriot in 1822.

After moving to New York City, Abell became acquainted with Azariah H. Simmons and William M. Swain, with whom he formed a business partnership to publish a penny paper.

They founded the Public Ledger in 1836 in Philadelphia, and a year later, Abell's partners agreed to back him when he proposed starting a penny paper in Baltimore, whose population at the time was 90,000.

"We have resolved upon the experiment of publishing a penny paper, entitled 'The Sun.' ... We shall strive to render it a channel of useful information to every citizen in every department of society whether literary, professional, mercantile, manufacturing or miscellaneous," wrote Abell and his two partners.

The birth of *The Sun* couldn't have come at a more inauspicious moment as the nation was reeling from the effects of the Panic of 1837, which had resulted in failed banks, inflation, shuttered factories and high unemployment.

At the time, Abell also faced formidable competition, as there were already six papers in the city -- the American, Chronicle, Gazette, Patriot, Republican and Transcript -- that sold for 6 cents a copy. There were also nine weeklies and two monthlies.

Unlike the stuffy and pompous newspapers being published in the city at the time, which were more reflective of opinion rather than hard news, Abell went in a different direction.

He assembled a team of reporters who were responsible for covering the courts, City Hall, meetings, police districts and anything else that was afoot that could be considered news.

Their efforts were very apparent when the first issue of *The Sun*, whose type most likely had been hand-set by Abell himself, came off the hand-operated press in a small building at 21 Light St. that served as the newspaper's first home.

The first edition of *The Sun* was four tabloid-sized pages. On Page 2, in a note to readers, Abell laid out what has remained the newspaper's enduring guiding philosophy and course for the past 175 years:

"We shall give no place to religious controversy, nor to political discussions of merely partisan character. On political principles, and questions involving the interest or honor of the whole country, it will be free, firm and temperate. Our object will be the common good, without regard to that of sects, factions or parties; and for this object we shall labor without fear or partiality. The publication of this paper will be continued for one year at least, and the publishers hope to receive, as they will try to deserve, a liberal support."

The 15,000 copies from Abell's initial press run went to every corner of the city.

The Sun made history four months after its founding when it printed, in its entirety, President Martin Van Buren's 12,000-word address to Congress. The text had been rushed to Baltimore by a courier aboard a fast-moving Baltimore & Ohio Railroad passenger train.

Abell was able to have the text set in type in time for the morning paper and was successful in beating the competition, which did not get the story until the next day.

On its first anniversary, *The Sun*'s circulation stood at an impressive 12,000, which forced Abell to move to a larger building at Gay and Baltimore streets.

Abell quickly embraced new technology that he envisioned would aid his news-gathering efforts and lead to a better paper.

It didn't take Abell long to see the possibilities in Samuel F.B. Morse's telegraph, invented in 1844. Abell later became a backer and supporter of the Magnetic Telegraph Co.

It was the Mexican War that placed *The Sun* on the national stage. In 1846, Abell set up a combination of telegraph, railroad, steamboat, stage coaches and a pony express line to speed war news to the city from New Orleans.

History was made again when *The Sun* ordered that President James K. Polk's Mexican War message to Congress be telegraphed to Baltimore in its entirety so it could be published.

From its beginning, *The Sun* had a Washington correspondent, a postal clerk who doubled as a reporter. By 1872, it had a full-fledged Washington Bureau at 1418 F St., later moving to a Gothic Victorian building of its own at 1317 F St., N.W. Eventually, more than 15 reporters worked in the Washington Bureau, covering the president and all avenues of the federal government.

The invention of the high-speed rotary press by New Yorker Richard Hoe in 1846 allowed *The Sun* to print 20,000 copies an hour, and the Linotype machine ended the drudgery of hand-setting type so that it could be done much faster.

A fleet of 500 carrier pigeons owned by Abell were also used for news gathering, speeding news to Baltimore from northern and southern cities, according to a book about the newspaper's first 150 years written by former Sunday editor Harold A. Williams.

Abell moved his paper in 1851 to an architecturally important building at Baltimore and South streets, which became known as *The Sun*

Iron Building. The cast-iron building had been designed by New York architect James Bogardus, and was the newspaper's home until the Baltimore Fire of 1904, which destroyed the building. No employees were killed.

The Civil War would enact a great strain on Abell and *The Sun*. While he was a Northerner, he sympathized with the South. When the city was occupied, he was warned that any pro-Confederate articles could lead to his arrest and charges of sedition.

Abell, also the largest holder of ground rents in Baltimore, had made substantial deposits in both Union and Southern banks, and by 1864 had bought out his original partners.

With the end of the Civil War, Abell editorially supported the re-enfranchisement of voters, the acceptance of African-Americans as freemen and President Andrew Johnson's plans for reconstruction of the South.

In the 1880s, Abell introduced telephones in the newsroom and business office of the newspaper, and the first typewriter made its appearance in 1893. No longer were reporters required to write their stories in longhand.

He lived to celebrate the 50th anniversary of *The Sun* and was 81 when he died at his residence at Charles and Madison streets, in 1888. His longtime friend Enoch Pratt, a Baltimore businessman who had been an advertiser from the paper's debut issue, said, "He has always been foremost in advocating all measures for the good of the city and of his fellow citizens."

After the Great Fire of 1904, *The Sun* erected a new building on the southwestern corner of Baltimore and Charles streets, where it remained until moving to its current home at 501 N. Calvert St. in 1950.

The paper was expanded on Oct. 6, 1901, when *The Sunday Sun* was first published, and again on April 18, 1910, with the birth of *The Evening Sun*.

Henry Louis Mencken joined *The Sun* in 1906 as Sunday editor, beginning a nearly 50-year career as a columnist, correspondent and adviser to the A.S. Abell Co.

The newspaper remained under control of the Abell family until 1910 when it was sold to Charles H. Grasty, who in turn sold the A.S.

Abell Co. in 1919 to Walter Abell 2nd, A.S. Abell's grandson, and Baltimore businessmen Van-Lear Black, Harry C. Black and R. Brent Keyser.

In 1939, the American Newspaper Guild won a representational election but a decade would pass before the Guild secured a contract with the company.

During World War II, war correspondents covered the war in the European and Pacific theaters. When the Japanese surrendered on the battleship USS Missouri, there were three Sunpaper war correspondents to witness the ceremony ¬-- Robert Cochrane, Thomas J. O'Donnell and Philip Potter.

Price Day, who was later editor-in-chief of The Sunpapers from 1960 to 1975, was the only war correspondent of an individual newspaper to witness the May 8, 1945, German surrender at Reims, France.

After the war, many changes came to the newspaper, including the expansion of foreign bureaus that stretched across the world from London to Tokyo. Locally, there were bureaus in the counties around Baltimore in addition to a State House Bureau in Annapolis.

At the time of *The Sun*'s 150th anniversary in 1987, the paper had correspondents in seven foreign capitals and news bureaus in addition to Washington, San Francisco and New York City.

The Sunday Sun Magazine, which grew out of a sepia-colored Sunday section commonly known as the Brown Section, was created in 1946 and continued publishing until 1996. After a 14-year absence, it resumed as a magazine in 2010.

The innovating spirit of A.S. Abell continued through the years. In 1975, the first computers entered the newsroom, which meant a switch from traditional "hot type" printing method. *The Sun* became one of the first large metropolitan dailies in the nation to do so.

The company purchased 60 acres at Port Covington in 1988, which had formerly been the yards of the Western Maryland Railway. The Hoe offset-presses that had printed the three papers at the Calvert Street plant since 1950 fell silent when the printing and packaging operations were transferred to Port Covington in 1992.

After 85 years, The Evening Sun rolled off the Port Covington presses for the last time on Sept. 15, 1995. A bold headline told the story:

"GOOD NIGHT, HON. Thanks for a great 85 years; will you love us in the morning?"

Many notable figures in American journalism have called *The Sun* and *Evening Sun* home, including:
-Russell Baker, writer;
-William Manchester, author and historian;
-Helen Delich Bentley, congresswoman;
-Sujata Massey, mystery writer;
-Jim McKay, sports broadcaster;
-Gwen Ifill, moderator and managing editor of "Washington Week";
-Louis Rukeyser, financial journalist and host of "Wall Street Week";
-Laura Lippman, mystery writer;
-David Simon, creator of TV's "The Wire" and "Homicide: Life on the Street."

In 1931, *The Sun* won the first of its 15 Pulitzer Prizes with and award to editorial cartoonist Edmund P. Duffy. He would eventually win two more.

In 1987, Alice Steinbach was the first female reporter at the paper to be presented a Pulitzer. Two more have since won: Lisa Pollack in 1997, and Diana K. Sugg in 2003.

Historic change arrived May 27, 1986

Thirty hours after the venerable News American folded on May 26, 1986, the A.S. Abell Co. ceased to exist after 149 years, when it was sold for $500 million to Times Mirror Co. of Los Angeles, publishers of the Los Angeles Times.

The Sun's first female managing editor in the paper's history, Kathryn Christensen, was named in 1991 to the paper's No. 2 position under John S. Carroll. She left two years later for "World News Tonight with Peter Jennings."

In 1996, the company launched Sunspot.net, its website, which since 2004 has been named baltimoresun.com.

Times Mirror was acquired in 2000 by Tribune Co. of Chicago, making *The Sun* a part of a major-market, multimedia company whose operations in addition to newspapers includes television and radio broadcasting, and interactive media.

In 2007, Tribune Co. was purchased by real estate tycoon Sam Zell, and the next year, the newspaper's 171-year-old name was changed to *The Baltimore Sun.* Many longtime Baltimoreans still refer to the newspaper as the Sunpapers.

Mary J. Corey, a former reporter and editor, became the first woman in the 173-year history of *The Baltimore Sun* to lead the newsroom, when she was named senior vice president and director of content in 2010.

Since 1837, Sun reporters have roamed the state chronicling news events that have shaped its destiny.

They have dutifully reported on governmental matters -- and at times scandals -- that affect the lives of all Marylanders. They have traveled from the shores of the Chesapeake Bay to far-flung corners of the world to bring readers accounts of historic breaking news events.

They have risked their lives covering wars, civil unrest and disasters. They have been eyewitnesses to the rise of the civil rights and women's movement. They have reported on assassinations, depressions, advancements in medicine, science, education, entertainment and technology, and every presidential administration from Martin Van Buren to Barack Obama. Today *The Sun* remains Maryland's dominant news organization, with the state's largest newspaper and a website that is among the most widely read in the Baltimore area.

Whether in print each morning, online throughout the day, on phones, iPads or other mobile devices, more people than ever read *The Sun* each day.

For 175 years, Sun reporters have held true to the mission first laid down by Arunah Shepherdson Abell.

Chapter Fifteen

Domino Sugar Corporation

Domino Sugar was established in 1922. For over ninety years the Baltimore Domino Sugar refinery has been supplying the key ingredient that helps bakers everywhere show their families how much they care.

Domino Sugar's Baltimore refinery is a state of the art facility that produces forty different products. It also manages twenty three packaging lines.

Baltimore's Domino Sugar company has the second highest sugar production capacity in the United States. It produces 885,000 tons of refined sugar a year.

A few times a month a giant tanker ship docks at the Domino plant unloading the raw sugar from the ship. It delivers ten million pounds of raw sugar per day usually it takes about a week to unload. The sugar travels by a conveyor belt swarming with feasting bees. It then goes to a massive hanger that can hold up to 100 million pounds of sugar in piles over 60 feet high.

One of the reasons for Domino's continued success may be harder to replicate its location. The refinery sits on the junction of Baltimore's Harbor. Its raw materials come in from Interstate 95. The B & O Railroad takes out its finished product.

The refined sugar is sent on rail cars to large industrial customers. Then it is shipped by truck to your local grocery store shelves.

Domino says, "Our strength is in our people." We have four hundred forty two employees at the refinery. Many employees are second and third generation Domino employees. We sustain an additional one hundred sixty-eight jobs through trucking, terminal operations, cargo handling, tugboat operators, and pilots. Our giant neon sign atop the refinery shows that Baltimore's Port is working. It is sixty one years old.

Fitz Gibbon is the refinery manager of the Domino Sugar plant in

Baltimore. Domino is the last major manu-
facturer still operating in Baltimore's Inner
Harbor. It wants to operate in Baltimore for
a number of reasons.

First they've updated their facilities, their
methods and their products. Second, their
location at the Inner Harbor is ideally suited
for the business. Finally, Domino and the
rest of the sugar industry have lobbied aggressively to maintain sugar price guarantees
from the federal government. This is done
to help American producers compete with
foreign rivals.

Much of the plant shows its age. Walls
and stairways are dingy with industrial
grime. Heavy steel fire doors have been in place since the 1920's. Some
of the original machinery is still in use. It processes 6.5 million pounds
of raw sugar a day.

The plant which recently invested two million in new clean air technology, presents a remarkable dichotomy between an aging industrial
behemoth and cutting-edge technological innovation.

Two of Domino's five boilers were installed when the plant switched
from fuel oil to natural gas in the early 2000's. Natural gas fuels an
on-site power plant with a seventeen, megawatt capacity that not only
powers the entire refinery, but is also capable of selling power back to the
grid.

They've also reduced the size of their workforce to about six hundred
from over 1,000 a generation ago. The company says they've done it
through attrition rather than layoffs.

"We've reduced the cost of operation by reducing energy consump-
tion." Fitz Gibbons said.

Domino's packaging warehouse looks nothing like the rest of the
refinery. High tech machinery spits out more than 359 billion single-serv-
ing sugar packets per year. The conveyor belt moves so fast you need a
strobe light to see the packets fly by.

CREDIT:
*By Domino Sugar - The Lafayette
advertiser. (Vermilionville [i.e.
Lafayette], La.), 21 June 1910.
Chronicling America: Historic
American Newspapers. Lib. of
Congress.*

Sugar packets are just one of the forty different final products retail and bulk the factory produces. Fitz Gibbon said the move to an array of value-added products is crucial to remaining profitable.

The refinery in Baltimore produces not just granulated, powdered, and brown sugars, but also flavored sugars. They also provide pharmaceutical grade sugars, and other specialty products in a variety of packaging's.

The plant in Baltimore is the only one in the country that produces sugar in retail sized plastic tubs as opposed to bags, eliminating the need for a sugar jar. They've been able to stay on the cutting edge of innovation. This made them remain competitive in this business said Jennifer Vey. She is a fellow at the Brookings Institution who has analyzed Baltimore.

The refinery has its own machine shop to make replacement parts for equipment that is long out of production. Melding these geriatric machines with their newer technology into a cohesive production unit is no easy feat.

"Making sugar is not like rocket science," said Ann Margaret Deavers. She is the environmental engineer at the Domino plant, although it actually is with all their modern equipment.

"We have a deep water berth with railroad and highway access. This is why throughout history you see wars over ocean access. It's a very valuable property. We don't want to give this up because somebody wants to build a condo with a view," said Fitz Gibbon.

The refinery is also less than two hours from Hershey, Pa. This is the home of one of their biggest and longest standing customers.

The average Domino employee in Baltimore makes $57,000 per year, plus benefits. Obviously this is significantly more than foreign sugar workers are paid. There are other economic advantages that have helped keep Domino here.

Unlike other major agricultural industries, sugar farmers and producers do not receive any direct payments from the U. S. government. They do however receive indirect subsidies in the form of price guarantees and limits on imported sugar. Domino and its competitors have lobbied and paid dearly to keep those subsides.

The stability of raw sugar and refined sugar prices gives them more business. This is more than they would have if they were thrown to the vagaries of the incredible volatile world market Roney said. I would argue it is extremely important to the survival of one of the last manufacturing operations in the port of Baltimore.

Domino's willingness to innovate its established supply chains and its accumulated capitol and expertise in the industry are what will keep it in Baltimore.

"You don't build a sugar refinery," Citing Domino's location and the nearly $1 billion cost of replicating its facilities. "You don't plop one down," said Fitz Gibbon.

None of that stopped Domino's parent company, American Sugar Refining from closing down. It was an even larger Domino refinery in Brooklyn in 2004. This happened soon after they acquired the Domino brand.

The larger a company gets, the more tenuous its ties become to its local branches. American Sugar Refining is the largest sugar company in the world.

Companies who left had nothing to do with their productivity. It was nothing to do with how good they were. Someone decided on a higher level to do this. They didn't want their company in Maryland any longer.

Domino's made over $9 million in capital improvements to the Baltimore plant in 2011. It seems Domino doesn't plan on going anywhere soon.

Chapter Sixteen

Bob Parsons

Bob Parsons was a typical teenage boy living in Baltimore in Highlandtown. His family struggled to make ends meet. He attended Pompei School in east Baltimore failing the fifth grade. He also went to high school in east Baltimore. He was a poor student in school with barely making it through high school. He worked a various odd jobs, from delivering newspapers, pumping gas, to factory work. He had it tough while growing up in east Baltimore. He worked for everything he has received; nothing was ever given to him.

Then he enlisted in the United States Marines Corps at age 17 and trained at Parris Island. Later he was assigned to the 26th Marine Regiment and went to Vietnam in 1969. He served as a rifleman and engaged in combat where he was seriously wounded; he spent months in the hospital recovering from his wounds. He received a Purple Heart along with the Combat Action Ribbon, and Vietnam Gallantry Cross. He tells everyone the Marine Corps taught him discipline, and how to handle responsibility. He says there's a right way to do things and a wrong way, so why not do it the right way.

Parsons says when you are in a combat situation it changes you forever. All the challenges I faced while in combat had a great impact on my life. The transition to civil life is not easy, most face emotional struggles.

After he recovered he completed his tour, and returned to Baltimore, he worked for a year in the Bethlehem Steel Mill. Then he enrolled in the University of Baltimore on a GI Bill. The same steel mill my father, Carmen, worked in. While in college he studied accounting. When it came time for him to graduate, he graduated Magna Cum Laude with a degree in accounting. Then he taught himself how to write code. He tells everyone the reason he turned his life around was because of the time he spent in the military.

He founded and sold a home accounting and software company, in his own home along with his former wife. His first company, Parsons Technology was a software company which he bought in 1984. He acquired it without any investors. He never borrowed any money, and when he sold the company to Intuit, Inc. in 1994 for $64 million, he kept most of the money. His ex-wife made out pretty well also.

He worked with established entrepreneurs. He took notes to see which one succeeded and why others failed. He paid close attention to them.

Then he started GoDaddy.com in 1997, a domain registrar and Web hosting company. Amazingly he started this company without any partners, no investors, and no loans; it then grew to 1,000 employees. Sadly Go Daddy nearly ended in failure. He invested $35 million of his own money to start the company. After he spent it all the way down to $6 million, he contemplated changing his career. Then suddenly the dot-com bubble burst. Overnight Go Daddy became solvent. It was the only company that could buy advertising and pay its bills. When they started doing this people began to notice them.

Of course there was controversy because of the racy commercials he made for Super Bowl Sunday. Parsons is not apologetic for his ads. He knows guys like to look at a well endowed woman. Guys noticed them when they are around so that's why I put them in my commercials. At first his ads received condemnation, but when his shares did this they went from 16 to 25 percent overnight.

Then Parsons sold 72 percent and stepped away from active involvement in 2011, the company was valued at more than $2 billion. He still remains the largest shareholder and serves on the board.

Veterans

Emotional struggles are often coupled with financial hardship, as veterans search for careers in a difficult job market. The veteran unemployment rate is 6.5 percent. For post-9/11 veterans, the rate is significantly higher, at 10.1 percent.

Parsons attempts to ease these transitions through his charitable donations and in the efforts of Go Daddy. Parsons has employed and worked closely with other veterans in his company. Parsons donates through his Go Daddy business to help veterans, his employees, and works closely with other veterans in his company.

KKR Co. who bought Go Daddy in 2011 actively recruits and hires veterans through its Vets at Work program. Go Daddy also offers counseling for veteran employees. A veteran is going to do a wonderful job because he or she understands responsibility.

Parsons started many companies, too many to mention. All of these companies added $100 million a year to his fortune. Today he is distributing his worth to his favorite causes. His favorite is the Semper Fi Fund which supports post 9/11 veterans from all branches of the military.

The Bob and Renee Parsons Foundation have supported several veterans' organizations. The Semper Fi Fund is one of them and has been supporting several veterans' organizations. It has also donated at least $10 million to the Southwest Center for HIV/Aids, helping it open its new center. Bob & Rene Parsons have a foundation to support this cause that was established in February 2012.

In December of 2013 they joined the Giving Pledge, an initiative started by Bill and Melinda Gates and Warren Buffett. It requires signatures to commit at least half of their fortunes to charity.

Motorcycles

Nowadays Parsons spends most of his time on the back of one of his 20 motorcycles. In2012 Parsons founded the Scottsdale, AZ based YAM Worldwide Inc. He owns Motorcycle dealerships of Harley-Davidson in Arizona, Mississippi, and Tennessee. They are Go AZ Motorcycles in Scottsdale, Arizona, Harley-Davidson of Scottsdale, Southern Thunder Harley-Davidson, Memphis, Tennessee, and Blues City Harley-Davidson, in Memphis, Tennessee. In April 2014, Parsons announced plans to build the "world's largest Harley-Davidson dealership" in Scottsdale.

Bob Parsons' 16 rules for survival

1. Get and stay out of your comfort zone. If you are worried about security it will drive you down.

2. Never give up. Nothing works the first time. If it was easy everyone would be doing it.

3. When you're ready to quit, you're closer than you think. Don't quit you are about to succeed.

4. With regard to whatever worries you, not only accept the worst thing that could happen, but make it a point to quantify what the worst thing could be. If it doesn't work they can't eat you.

5. Focus on what you want to have happen. As you think so you shall be.

6. Take things a day at a time. Don't look too far ahead.

7. Always be moving forward. Small daily improvements eventually result in huge advantages.

8. Be quick to decide. A good plan executed is better than a perfect plan today.

9. Measure everything of significance. Anything that is measured and watched improves.

10. Anything that is not managed will deteriorate. Look closely to areas you haven't checked for a while and you will find the problem.

11. Pay attention to your competitors, but pay more attention to what you're doing. Remember everything looks good from a distance.

12. Never let anybody push you around. You have just as much right to what you are doing.

13. Never expect life to be fair. Life isn't fair. You make your own breaks.

14. Solve your own problems. A wise man keeps his own counsel.

15. Don't take yourself too seriously. None of us are in control as much as we think we are.

16. There's always a reason to smile. Life is short.

Golf

In September 2013 Mr. Parsons purchased the Golf Club in Scottsdale. It is a 292 acre members-only golf course, for $600,000 and undisclosed debt, and renamed it Scottsdale National Golf Club. In 2014 Parsons purchased undeveloped properties adjacent to his golf course including a 223 acre parcel for a reported $55 million. It is a 41 acre parcel for $5.4 million and a smaller tract for $2.3 million. Also in 2014, Parsons announced plans to build a new clubhouse, nine-hole practice facility. It also had a second 18-hole golf course on the property. In January 2015, Parsons launched Parsons Xtreme Golf (PXG), a high-end golf club manufacturing company. That same month, professional golfer Ryan Moore used prototype PXG irons and wedges when he played in the Hyundai Tournament of Champions. It is a PGA Tour event. PXG is expected to launch a full line of golf equipment including drivers, fairway woods, hybrids, irons, wedges and putters.

Real Estate Holdings

Since 2012, YAM Properties has purchased more than 675,000 square feet of commercial real estate in Arizona's Valley of the Sun region. YAM properties include: Scottsdale Grayhawk Center, Retail and office projects Citadelle Plaza and II Palazzo, Arrowhead Professional Center, McDowell Mountain Market place, Centerpoint on Mill, Hayden Station, and The Cornerstone shopping center and many retail space in two properties.

The Bob & Rene Parsons Foundation

In 2012, Bob and Renee Parsons awarded over $64 million to more than 62 charities and organizations worldwide. Bob Parsons has resigned his position as executive chairman at Go Daddy in order to devote more time to his other interests. Renee manages the foundation on a day-to-day basis. A third of the money is awarded to local Arizonian charities.

Because of the Giving Pledge the Buffett's, and the Gates created, the Parsons accepted to donate half their wealth to charity. Since its inception the foundation has donated over $10 million on a yearly basis placing it among the state's 10 biggest givers.

During 2012-2014, the foundation donated over $72 million, and its assets amount to more than $9.5 million. After the 2010 Haiti earthquake the Parsons visited, the foundation pledging $500 thousand for Hope in Haiti. They also donated a further $4 million towards relief efforts.

It has inspired hope by providing critical funding at critical times to communities striving to make a difference.

Chapter Seventeen

Ed Polochick

Ed Polochick is the Artistic Director of concert Artist of Baltimore. He is the maestro who conducts a professional orchestra with an all-professional vocal ensemble. It has seventy musicians that are celebrating their 30th season.

From 1979 to 1998 Mr. Polochick was on the conducting staff of the Baltimore Symphony Orchestra. He was the director of the Symphony Chorus. He also was the founder and director of the Baltimore Symphony Chorus Chamber Singers. When he is in Baltimore he is the guest conductor. During his tenure with the BSO, he established annual Holiday Pops and Messiah performances. These concerts have remained a Baltimore holiday tradition for nearly three decades.

In the summer 1987, Mr. Polochick was conductor of the Musicisti Americani Summer Festival in Sulmona, Italy. In the autumn of the same year, he conducted the Peabody Symphony Orchestra in Moscow. It was the first appearance of an American student orchestra in the Soviet Union. In recognition of the Moscow tour, Mr. Polochick received an ASCAP Award of Adventurous Programming of American Music.

In 2000 Mr. Polochick received the Peggy and Yale Gordon Achievement Award. He was made an honorary member of the Baltimore Music Club. Two years later he was awarded the coveted Johns Hopkins University Distinguished Alumnus Award. In 2004 he was named Baldwin Scholar at the University of Notre Dame of Maryland. He holds lectures, demonstrations and panels on the creative act of music. He was awarded the Keys to the City by Lincoln's Mayor Coleen Seng in 2007. In 2010 he received a commission from Nebraska Governor David Heineman as an Admiral in the Nebraska Navy. In 2011 he was the only American to serve as an adjudicator for the Rosa

Ponselle International Vocal Competition in Collazo, Italy.

Mr. Polochick is frequently asked to share his knowledge and love of music at various lecture series, adjudications and radio broadcasts. Each year renowned broadcaster, Marc Steiner, invites him to co-host his radio program in Baltimore. It is a celebration of the holiday season music. He is also a regular panelist on Face the Music, a radio review program of recordings hosted by Jonathan Palevsky of WBJC-FM, Baltimore. For nearly two decades, he and Mr. Palevsky have been co-hosting WBJC's annual Christmas Program.

Although Mr. Polochick resides in Baltimore, he considers Lincoln to be his second home. On each visit he contributes to the community through LSO's public performances, school visits, workshops, master classes, and other educational activities.

Edward Polochick has been the Music Director of Lincoln's Symphony Orchestra since 1998. He has expanded LSO's music series through innovative classical music programs. He also holds family concerts, pops concerts, and July 4th events like the Uncle Sam Jam. In addition to his role with LSO, he serves as Artistic Director of Concert Artists. He founded a professional chamber orchestra and vocal ensemble of eighty musicians in 1987. On each visit he contributes to the community through LSO's public performances, school visits, workshops, master classes, and other educational activities. He makes classical music accessible to everyone in Lincoln.

Maestro Polochick has served on the faculty of the Peabody Conservatory of Music in Baltimore since 1979. He serves in a multitude of conducting positions including Associate Conductor of Orchestras, Director of Choral Ensembles, and Opera Conductor. Not only is he widely recognized as a conductor, but he is an award-winning pianist and harpsichordist. He regularly conducts from the keyboard with Concert Artist, the Baltimore Symphony Orchestra, and Lincoln's Symphony Orchestra. He has also appeared as piano soloist with the Philadelphia Orchestra and the Los Angeles Chamber Orchestra under the direction of Sir Neville Marriner.

Since winning the first Leopold Stokowski Conducting Award in 1978 he continues to attract world-wide attention as an orchestral, choral, and operatic conductor. Because of this award he conducts the Philadelphia Orchestra. In addition to conducting the Philadelphia and Baltimore Symphony Orchestras, his guest appearances include the Houston Symphony, Chautauqua Symphony, the Opera Company of Philadelphia, Omaha Symphony, Jacksonville Symphony, Charleston (SC) Symphony Orchestra, Aalborg Symphony (Denmark), Daejeon Philharmonic (South Korea), St. Petersburg Symphony (Russia), and the State of Mexico Symphony Orchestra (Mexico).

With all these accomplishments under his belt, he is still a local resident of Baltimore. His home is located in East Baltimore across the street of Patterson Park. He is also a very familiar customer at Sabatino's.

I have interviewed people who know Mr. Polochick and here are some of the things they told me about him.

Annabel Wherley is one of the performers in the chorus and this is what she told me about Mr. Polochick. He is a musical genius. When she auditioned for the part in the chorus she was nervous. He came with her even though the audition lasted an hour. He even coached her.

He understands singing and mostly the act of singing. He knows what is required to make a beautiful sound. He knows how to conduct a chorus in a way that supports the singers. This is unusual in a musical conductor.

The Concert Artists con Sympatric Coral and Concert artists of Baltimore sang with the Temple choir, the Temple University and the Philadelphia Orchestra. They have worked with many famous conductors but none of them are like him. He is enthusiastic and because of this he energizes his group.

When the chorus is performing his facial expressions are beautiful. The only thing wrong about this is that the audience can't see this because his back is towards them. People should be able to see this by the way he moves. It is a wonderful thing to share as a singer performing. This is why she sings in the choir. The communication Mr. Ed has with the singers is outstanding.

Here is another point of view about Mr. Polochick from a person who attends many of Mr. Polochick's concerts.

Father Robert Albright, along with his friends, Jim and Saundra Hintenach, M's. Lynn Hall and Sister Patricia Nightingale, have all attended many of Mr. Polochick's performances of The Messiah. Father Albright told me the production Mr. Polochick performs of the Messiah is by far the best he has heard. The period of the Baroque music which includes Bach, Handel, and Vivaldi, is meant to be played fast. They wrote fast music because that's authentic to the period it was written in. Other conductors play it slow but Mr. Polochick gives it life because this music was written quickly and that is how it is meant to be played. Father Albright says it is the best production of the music in the world.

Father Albright also said Mr. Polochick is truly an icon of Baltimore because of the way he performs music. Mr. Polochick is so human and that's something that should be said about him. Most conductors do not have the attitude or demeanor Mr. Polochick has on or off the stage. He is a genuine nice person.

When Fr. Albright went back stage to meet Mr. Polochick after one of his performances, Fr. Albright told Mr. Polochick he must be exhausted. Mr. Polochick replied no; on the contrary I'm energized. Music brings him to life and he brings music to life. He is a people person, his personality is fabulous.

In 2000 Mr. Polochick received the Peggy and Yale Gordon Achievement Award and was made an honorary member of the Baltimore Music Club. Two years later he was awarded the coveted Johns Hopkins University Distinguished Alumnus Award. In 2004 he was named Baldwin Scholar at the University Of Notre Dame of Maryland where he held lectures, demonstrations and panels on the creative act of music.

He was awarded the Keys to the City by Lincoln's Mayor Coleen Seng in 2007, and in 2010 received a commission from Nebraska Governor David Heineman as an Admiral in the Nebraska Navy. In 2011 he was the only American to serve as an adjudicator for the Rosa Ponselle International Vocal Competition in Calazzo, Italy.

Mr. Polochick is frequently asked to share his knowledge and love of music at various lecture series, adjudications and radio broadcasts.

Each year renowned broadcaster, Marc Steiner, invites him to co-host his radio program in Baltimore celebrating music of the holiday season. He is also a regular panelist on Face the Music, a radio review program of recordings hosted by Jonathan Palevsky of WBJC-FM, Baltimore. For nearly two decades, he and Mr. Palevsky have been co-hosting WBJC's annual Christmas Program.

Iconic Baltimore Business:
H&S Bakery

CHAPTER EIGHTEEN

H & S Bakery

The story of H & S Bakery is a classic American success story. It starts with the Paterakis and Tsakalos families, who came from Greece to make a new and better life for their families. Isadore "Steve" Paterakis came to America in 1921. He sent for his wife, Kyriaki, and their daughters, Despina and Liberty in 1928. After Mr. Paterakis' family came to America, their son John Paterakis, Jr. was born.

Harry's family, Nicholas and Rodanthi, moved to Vandergrift, PA. from Greece. Harry was born on February 17, 1919. His family moved to Baltimore in 1936. Harry lived through the Great Depression and World War II; he knew hard work has its rewards.

Mr. Harry worked as a truck driver for Athens Bakery located on South Bouldin Street. This is where he met Isidore "Steve"Paterakis who was a baker there. It was through Steve that Harry met his future wife, Steve's daughter, Liberty Paterakis. Harry Tsakalos married Liberty Paterakis, bringing the two families together. The couple married in 1942 and they had their only child Nicholas the following year.

In the early days they worked out of a bakery on a South Fagley Street's row house. Harry was friends with my Grandfather Gaitano Di Pietro. Gaitano became ill and back in those days pneumonia was a serious illness. The doctors didn't have a cure for it. Many people died from the disease. Because Gaitano was ill he took Harry around and introduced him to some of the people he sold bread to in Highlandtown.

Then Harry and Steve purchased Olga and Son Bakery in East Baltimore in 1943 and opened their new bakery for business. They reopened the company under the name H&S after themselves, the "H" being for Harry and the "S" for Steve. They started making Italian bread by hand and baking it in an old brick flat-hearth oven. Steve along with his wife Kyriaki and their son John made the bread. Harry drove the company's sole delivery truck, handling all the wholesale and home delivery service.

When Steve Paterakis died in 1953 from complications of leukemia, his son John Paterakis who was only 23 at the time inherited his father's interest in the bakery. He became the vice president of sales and marketing of the H&S firm. He did this along with Harry and both of them continued to grow the business. The H&S bakery grew into one of the largest bakers on the East Coast. They produced more than 100 varieties of breads, rolls and specialty items. H&S Bakery was incorporated in 1962 and set their sights on a rapid growth.

The family continued to grow when John Paterakis wed Antoinette Apostolou. A new generation of six children came along after this and the company continued to grow. Their four sons Steve, Bill, John and Chuck work with their father in the business today. Harry's son Nicholas and his three grandsons Harry, Michael, and Christopher continue as the third generation working for the company. Harry and Liberty also have great-grandchildren Nicholas, Jacob, Mixalitsa and Elijah.

Neither H&S Bakery with all its extensive divisions and holdings, nor its family members have strayed from their Baltimore roots. Steve and Harry have always been humble people and beloved by the community, and especially by their employees. This statement has been repeated more and more by not only their family members, but also their employees. They have always taken pride in their achievements.

Harry would often meet the bread deliverers and route salesmen as they brought their trucks back to the Southeast Baltimore plant. He was a hand on man who managed the plant. He helped settle their daily accounts. He was also the treasurer of the business. He had a good head for business. He was a humble giant who had a heart of gold. Harry and Liberty worked so much; they ate out every night dressed in their work clothes. They often came to Sabatino's for dinner because it was close for them to come. Mr. Harry was a generous person with a big heart and kind as he could be.

Liberty and Harry had such great work ethics they taught their family the commitment and importance of hard work, dedication to the community and pride of achievement. Liberty was a strong woman working in a man's world. She was the last woman in the extended Paterakis and Tsakalos families to have worked at the bakery. This was a custom for the men of the traditional Greek family. John Paterakis Jr. also told the rest of his family this.

H&S moved to Fells Point and expanded a plant along Fleet and Bond streets in the 1960's. They continue to make bread in the traditional European flavor and crust. It produces hearth baked bread, rolls bagels, English Muffins, and cinnamon buns. The appetizing and fabulous aromas that waft through the neighborhood streets of the City are fabulous.

The family also answered a request of then Mayor William Donald Schaefer to help with the development of Harbor East. John Paterakis was a visionary leader focused on growing Baltimore, and his impact can be seen throughout the City. John Paterakis helped redevelop part of the downtown harbor. A good portion of this area became Harbor East, developing the Marriott Waterfront Hotel as well as the Four Seasons Hotel. Along with his development company, H&S Properties Development Corporation, he also built Courtyard by Marriott, and offices for Sylvan Learning Systems, Inc. and Fidelity and Guaranty Life Insurance Company. Liberty and Harry moved from their row home on Highland Avenue, which was right near my home in Highlandtown. They moved to one of the new and improved developed condos in Harbor East.

In the 1960's John Paterakis and Ray Kroc shook hands and created the Northeast Foods. It became a state of the art bakery division. In 1965, the Athens Automatic Rolls plant opened in Baltimore as Northeast Foods' a fully automated rolls plant in East Baltimore. It is located at the same site Esskay meat packing plant use to be located. Northeast Foods and H&S Bakery continue to thrive because its people shared Harry & Steve's same core values of hard work, dedication to community and pride of achievement.

It has become one of the largest bakeries on the East Coast. It bakes more than 100 varieties of breads, rolls and specialty items. Their sister business also owned by the Paterakis-Tsakalos family, Northeast Foods Inc., has been a supplier to McDonald's hamburger rolls since 1965. They have a fleet of more than 200 tractor trailers. H&S has gone from a three-employee shop into a baking empire. John Paterakis always called himself "Just a little Greek baker who got lucky." He donated too many politicians which sometimes cause him conflicts. He was a businessman who was totally self-made. He was a man who had very special skills for both cultivating important customers and delivery and outstanding product. He had a vision beyond the bakery to improve Baltimore.

Now that Mr. Paterakis and Mr. Nick have passed their children and grand children run the business for them today.

Bill Paterakis is the head of Northeast Food which is a subsidiary of H&S Bakery. John J. Paterakis, Jr. heads the sales department. Chuck Paterakis is in charge of transportation and construction. Steve Paterakis runs the Schmidt baking division.

All three of Mr. Nick Tsakalos work for H&S Bakery today also since he passed away.

CHAPTER NINETEEN

Kevin Plank

Kevin Plank was born August 13, 1972 in Kensington, Maryland. He is the youngest of five boys who grew up there.

He later walked onto the University of Maryland football team after college recruiters passed over him. He turned himself into a special team's bruiser. He eventually became captain of the special team for the Terrapins.

Sitting in a packed locker room after games, he noticed his teammates were all wearing heavy, sweat-soaked shirts. The initial idea for Under Armour came from Plank being tired of having to change out of the sweat-soaked T-shirts he wore under his jersey. Plank was the sweatiest guy on the football field.

After graduation, Plank searched for synthetic moisture-wicking fabric for athletic performance. He looked for a fabric to make him lighter and faster. After seven prototypes, Plank decided on a material. He searched tailor shops in College Park, Maryland. He even went to the garment district in New York and had shirts made, and the company took off. He came up with a lightweight sweat wicking shirt using fabrics from women's undergarments.

While he attended the University of Maryland, he launched various businesses of his own. Plank developed Cupid's Valentine; he sold roses for Valentine's Day. He saved $17,000 from the rose business. He eventually used this money to start Under Armour. Plank graduated from Maryland in 1996 with a bachelor's degree in business administration. He started his business in the basement of his grandmother's Georgetown row house back in 1999.

He asked his former team mates to try on the shirt. He told them it was different from the cotton T-shirt. When his friends went on to play professional football, he sent them T shirts and asked them to pass

John Musotto & Kevin Plank.

them on to the other players. He advertised in ESPN, the Magazine for $25,000 in 1999. The add brought him direct sales up to $1 million. He lied to early customers to make the company sound bigger than it was.

He developed and maintained personal relationships with a network of 50 to 60 friends from college who went to play in the NFL. The connection with his friends helped him to expand his company. He sent them each three shirts and asked them to try them. He asked them to try the T-shirts. He said if they liked them, give one to each guy in the locker next to you.

In 2003 Under Armour had their first advertisement on TV. The commercial featured his team mate Eric Ogbogu shouting "we must protect this house." This quote can be heard throughout many colleges over and over again today. The company's revenues passed the $1 billion mark in 2010. Plank's net worth was estimated by Forbes magazine at $1.05 billion. In 2012 Plank was recognized by Forbes for changing the athlete's playing field and was named #3 on Forbes list. In April 2015 Plank's net worth was estimated at $3.5 billion.

Plank has been a long-time supporter of the University of Maryland's Robert H. Smith School of business and Dingman Center for Entrepreneurship. He is also responsible for the development of the annual Cupid's Cup business competition. The competition got its name from Plank's "Cupid's Valentine"rose business he began while attending the University.

Plank is also active within the Baltimore and Washington D.C. communities sitting on the Board of Directors for the Baltimore City Fire Foundation, the Greater Baltimore Committee and Greater Washington Sports Alliance. He is also a member of their Board of Trustees for Living Classrooms.

When Kevin Plank gave a talk at the University of Maryland to the graduates he told them to have passion in whatever they do. He told them it was passion that enabled him to turn Under Armour into the company it is today. I didn't have someone to show me how it was done. The one thing I had was passion. Passion helped me to make the idea for a T-shirt become a reality.

Plank continues to support the university since he graduated twenty years ago. He contributed $25 million toward the transformation of Cole Field House into an indoor practice facility.

Patrick Ronk, a graduating senior who served as two-time student body president gave a speech. He told his fellow students, "It's great that we have a commencement speaker who is not only famous but who cares so much about the university. He is a Terp himself. Many schools get big names but they aren't attached to the school as much as Kevin is and that's why he's special.

Under Armour founder Kevin Plank made his millions as the underdog competitor to Nike and he's now bringing the heat to Silicon Valley. Despite Plank's bold $710 million purchase of a trio of health and fitness tracking apps, Under Armors' stock was up more than 40% midway through 2015. He also bought a $475 million on a calorie counting app, My Fitness Pal. His lofty goal created the world's best digital health platform to rival Google, Apple, Jawbone, and Fit bit.

Under Armour is now America's second biggest sportswear vendor behind Nike.

Kevin's ten rules for success

First: We control our own destiny.
Second: Perfection is the enemy of innovation.
Third: Don't get complacent, don't get lazy.
Fourth: Find your Darth Vader.
Fifth: Why not me – there might be someone better.
Sixth: Work with great people.
Seven: Be famous for one thing.
Eight: Make fast decisions.
Nine: Have fight like family mentality.
Tenth: Give it a shot; don't let anyone talk you out of it.

He also said you are never too old.

The booming company has grabbed the sports world's attention with its latest deal in college apparel. UCLA and Under Armour have agreed to a fifteen year, $280 million contract. It will push both organizations to the top of the escalating and lucrative college apparel business. The deal is the largest in NCAA history and signals a switch for UCLA, which was recently an Adidas school. The Bruins will retain creative control over their uniforms but want Under Armour to come in and help spice up fan apparel. They may also allow their new partners a shot at designing an alternative football uniform.

Under Armour already have deals with Auburn, Wisconsin and Notre Dame. Plank told the Times the move was an attempt "to plant our flag in L.A." Under Armour is still a relatively fresh player when it comes to nabbing league superstars. Nonetheless, the company signed two-time MVP Steph Curry in a deal some are reporting worth up to $14 billion. This happened for the 20 year old company. Curry was under contract with Nike but the company made several missteps to resign him. This allowed Under Armour to scoop up the point guard who has developed into one of the league's best players.

The company has made deals with Berkeley and now Los Angeles. They are showing their interest for expansion in the college game. Under

Armour has also signed a deal with Notre Dame. Maryland is currently paired with the growing companies. Nike and Adidas still dominate the college market.

Kevin recently opened a store in Chicago and is opening two hundred more stores today. Once you have his products you wondered how you ever lived without them. There are two hundred engineers working on building the next product. It is a shoe that has a chip in it that lets you know how far you went.

He is creating data to make our lives better. With this apt it can make people smarter and feel better about themselves. It will give people the power to be strong. He created a partnership with SAP. It will help to enrich lives.

He wants to build a youth center were the Riots took place in April of 2015. He is building a recreation center there for the youth. He donated ten million to Johns Hopkins women's breast health center. He made it possible to find the women's section without walking all over the hospital to find it.

He has passion. He built a great product and built a great team. Kevin has said, "It's what you do in the dark that matters in the light, which puts you in the light." What does it take to be a champion? He had the insight to pursue his dream. He created a product that helped football players be warm in the winter. It also helped the baseball players be cool in the summer.

His business is located today where the Sam's Club was located. He made his company a five hundred company. He wants to grow things great for Baltimore. He is going to build a twenty four acre of land to fifty acres and make it be Baltimore's front porch. He plans to do this in ten to twenty years.

He is going to make innovation labs. He wants to make it be possible to live, work, and play and be inspired here. We want the City to be great and hope Under Armour can make it that way. He said Our House is just getting started.

Kevin released his first batch of Sagamore Spirit a new straight rye whiskey on May 13th. This happened right in time for the Preakness Stakes. At Plank's Sagamore Farm the co-founder Bill McDermond hosted a party for the rye whiskey on May 19th.

Plank's remarks were on video because he was giving the commencement address at his alma mater, the University of Maryland. He bought Sagamore a horse breeding farm of Pimlico from the owner and president Albert Vanderbilt II in 2007.

A distillery for Sagamore Spirit is under construction in the Port Covington section of Baltimore. It is expected to open by early 2017. The rye that is currently aged out of state is cut to 83 proofs with spring water. The spring water bubbles up through the limestone on Plank's farm. It is kind of a sweet rye.

Plank's firm Sagamore Ventures is expected to buy Harbor Boating Inc. The city agrees to award the firm another long term contract. It will operate passenger service around the Inner Harbor, with stops in Fells Point, Canton and other waterfront spots. Sagamore hopes to expand the water taxi, adding new boats, longer hours, more stops, and an on-demand offering in partnership with Uber. Under Armour already partially funds the city's free Harbor Connector commuter boat service.

The water taxis plays a large role in the plans for Plank's massive mixed-use development in Port Covington. What we really want to do is make this a truly commuter-friendly service, said Demian Costa. She is the managing partner of Sagamore Ventures, Plank's venture capital firm.

Laurie Schwartz, president of the nonprofit Waterfront Partnership, said Sagamore would offer creative ideas and better technology to make water transportation more attractive. It'll bring a new sense of energy, a new infusion of capital and new creativity for how Baltimore can best operate a water transit system, Laurie said. They're looking at it not only as a business investment but as a way to serve the city better.

Harbor boating plans to expand water taxi hours, with the aim of starting service at 6am and operating until late at night. The operator plans to create nine new stops, including in Port Covington and Cherry Hill, for a total of 21. Michael Middleton said adding stops in those neighborhoods shows Plank's commitment to residents who live around the site of the proposed development. Trying to keep your ticket price low is difficult because there's a fine line between too much money and not enough money. The boats will be bigger and able to carry about 50 people. There will also be smaller boats to fit a dozen people hailed by Uber. There also will be tracking devices so riders can see when they were arriving. The new business will be hiring up to 150 people during the peck seasons. Most of these people will be from Baltimore.

Kevin Plank has been an inspiration to me and all of Baltimore.

The famous restaurant where the famous meet

Peachy's FAVORITE Recipes

CRAB CAKES

1 lb. of crab meat
1 tsp. Old Bay seasoning
1 tbsp. mayonnaise
2 slices white bread with the crust removed,
    broken into small pieces
1 tbsp. chopped parsley
1 egg beaten

Mix all the ingredients together and form into a cake. Fry quickly until golden.

PIZZELLE COOKIES

My Mom's Pizzelle Cookies:

6 large eggs
1 ¾ cups of sugar
1 cup of butter
½ bottle vanilla extract
½ bottle anise extract
3 ½ cups all purpose flour
1 teaspoon baking powder
Spray oil on the iron as needed
Powdered sugar

Beat eggs at medium speed, add sugar, beating until thick, add butter, vanilla, and anise. Mix well; add flour and baking soda and beat until smooth. Spray pizzelle iron and heat for 2 minutes. Place 1 teaspoon of dough on each cookie plate, and close iron. Cook for 30-40 seconds until desired color. Sprinkle cookies with powdered sugar before the cookies are cooled off. Makes 3 ½ dozen cookies..

CRAB SOUP

1 lb. of crab meat	½ tsp. salt
3 ham hocks	4 tbsp. Old Bay seasoning
4 cups of chicken broth	3 cups chopped celery
1 large onion peeled & diced	2 – 3 large bags frozen mixed
6 baby carrots	vegetables
2 cups cabbage, chopped	1 large potato, peeled
4 tbsp. parsley	and cut in cubes
1 tsp. pepper	1 - 8 oz. can tomato puree

Fill an 8 qt. pot with water. Add all the ingredients except the vegetables, and let these ingredients cook. After it comes to a boil, turn it down and let it simmer for 1 hour. Add all the vegetables and crab meat and cook for 2 more hours. Serves 10

APPLE PIE

The crust:	*The filling:*
2 ½ cups flour	6 apples peeled and diced
1 cup butter	½ cups brown sugar
8 tbsp. water	½ cups sugar
	2 tbsp. butter

For Crust: Roll out the dough and put in pan. Add all the ingredients and then bake.

For Filling: Sprinkle cinnamon & sugars generously over the apples. Pat butter evenly over the apples. Bake at 450 degrees for 15 minutes. Turn oven to 350 degrees for 45 minutes. Cook in oven till the crust is lightly brown. When you take the pie out of the oven rub some butter on top of the pie.

BEAN SOUP

1 lb. bag of dry Navy Beans

3 ham hocks

4 cups of chicken broth

3 cups of chopped celery

1 lg. onion peeled and
  chopped

3 tsp. oregano

4 tbsp. parsley

1 tsp. pepper

½ tsp. salt

Wash the beans and let them soak for about 1 hr. Add water in an 8 qt. pot. Add all the ingredients. Bring to boil and let cook.

CHICKEN SOUP

3 chicken thighs deboned and
  skinless (they have the
  sweetest meat)

12 qt. pot of water

1 lge. onion cut in half, and
  then into smaller pieces

8 stalks of celery cut in half,
  then cut in thirds (with
  the leaves on as they have
  more flavor)

30 baby carrots
  peeled and cut in half

1 tbsp. of salt

1/3 tsp. of pepper

4 tbsp. parsley

1 - 8 oz. can of tomato puree

1 lb. bag of egg noodles

2 cans of chicken broth

Cook the chicken in 12 qts. water. Add salt and pepper, and chicken broth. After water comes to a boil lower and cook for one hour. Add the tomato puree, and cook for another hour. In a pot of boiling water, cook the egg noodles until tender, strain the noodles. Remove the chicken and shred it. Put the chicken back into the soup and add the noodles. Add grated cheese to your taste. Serves 6.

Jack Tar Potatoes

Bake a potato and after it is baked open it up and scoop all the potato out of the skin add a large scoop of sour cream, a little bit of parsley, a small hand of grated cheese, a small amount of bacon bits, and a couple pats of butter. Mix all these ingredients together in bowl, then put everything back into the potato skin and bake for another ten minutes. It is the most delicious potato you will ever taste.

Shrimp Renato

Peel and devein the shrimp. Cook in light brandy and wine sauce with butter and extra virgin olive oil. Only cook the shrimp for a few minutes; the longer you cook the shrimp, the harder it becomes. Then melt some cheese & prosciutto ham over it. The sauce is delicious.

Big Renato the father of little Renato, who is also the other owner of Sabatino's created this dish when his son Little Renato was born. Little Renato is now in his forties.

Lima Bean Soup

1 lb. bag dry Lima Beans	4 tbsp. parsley
3 ham hocks	1 large onion, peeled &
4 cups of chicken broth	chopped
3 cups chopped celery	½ tsp. salt
3 tsp. oregano	¼ tsp. pepper

Wash the beans and let them soak for about 1 hour. Add water in an 8 qt. pot. Add all the ingredients. Bring to a boil and let cook for 2½ hours. Shred the meat and add it to the soup. Serves 10.

Edgar Allan Poe's grave at Westminster and Burying Ground in downtown Baltimore.

Fort McHenry